# UNLOCKING A BROKEN WORLD

a story of discovery

SCOTT & CONNIE PAYNE

WestBow
PRESS®
A DIVISION OF THOMAS NELSON
& ZONDERVAN

WestBow Press books may be ordered through booksellers or by contacting:

WestBow Press
A Division of Thomas Nelson & Zondervan
1663 Liberty Drive
Bloomington, IN 47403
www.westbowpress.com
1 (866) 928-1240

Front and back cover images provided by ©Life & Peace Photography.

ISBN: 978-1-9736-1551-4 (sc)
ISBN: 978-1-9736-1553-8 (hc)
ISBN: 978-1-9736-1552-1 (e)

Library of Congress Control Number: 2018900821

Print information available on the last page.

WestBow Press rev. date: 8/27/2021

# DEDICATION

To the wonderful prayer warriors, volunteers, and supporters of Inner City Mission, including businesses, churches, and organizations: You have carried us through many precious, yet sometimes difficult moments in homeless ministry. To you, we offer this book as a labor of love for your many years of faithfulness. Thank you from the bottom of our hearts.

# ACKNOWLEDGMENTS

To the Inner City Mission board of directors and staff members, past and present, we are indebted to you, and amazed. You have shared our vision and waited patiently on us for years, staying the course. Your compassion for the homeless and years of service made *Unlocking a Broken World* possible. Thank you for trusting us, loving us, and giving us the freedom to write this story.

To our friends at CLASSeminars, thank you for making us believe we could actually write. Gerry Wakeland and Linda Gilden, your leadership skills and encouragement inspired us to persevere through all things. Gloria Penwell, you spoke words of wisdom into our lives when we needed it most. Larry Leech, your coaching skills truly enlightened our writing. Ron Benson and Lee Warren, your On Ramp sessions and manuscript advice were invaluable. We appreciate all of you for making our venture into writing possible.

To our six children and their spouses, Rachel (Seth), Joshua (Nikki), Caleb (Bethany), Sarah, Jacob (Taylor) and Isaac (Allison), and to our grandchildren, Isabelle, Addison, Sophia, Corey, Liam, Ella, Daniel (in heaven), Malachi, Sayla, Zion, and baby Anna, we are so grateful for you. You understood our time limitations and loved us anyway. Words cannot express how blessed and honored we feel to have you in our lives. Thank you for living this story with us and for carrying the torch to the next generation.

To our parents, Allen and Deletta Payne and Gene and Larita Gillespie, thank you for sacrificing and shaping our lives forever. Gene and Larita, you celebrate life in heaven now, but you left a wonderful example of tenacity and hard work. Allen and Deletta, your gift for hospitality is beyond compare. Thank you for loving us unconditionally, and for always making us feel important.

To Life & Peace Photography, (a.k.a. our daughter-in-law, Bethany Payne), thank you for artistically capturing a broken world through photography. Your talents and flair for detail made our vision for the cover of *Unlocking a Broken World* come to life. Thank you for your willingness to trek the banks of the Sangamon River bluffs with Connie (and Corey) to find the perfect spot for the cover photo. We are also grateful for the author pic and the many book titles you suggested, including the one we chose.

To Larry Crossett of Midwest Journey Services, thank you for helping us design a book cover that creatively balances graphics, text, and colors. Your skills and patience brought all the pieces together. Thank you for your friendship and for your faithfulness in designing the many brochures, booklets, and other publications for Inner City Mission through the years.

To the Inner City Mission Strategic Team members, TyLinda Blackstock, Jeff Higginson (in heaven), Becky Payne (LCPC) and Dennis Petty (LCSW), thank you for sharing your insight, education, and experiences in all those endless meetings we had. Together, we laid out strategies for tackling homelessness at its core—strategies we still use today. Thank you for your wisdom, for the laughs, and for helping ICM build a solid foundation for helping the homeless.

To the former residents of Inner City Mission who are featured in this book, thank you for allowing us to write your stories. Your names remain anonymous, but you are forever etched in our memory. Your lives played a vital role in our understanding of homelessness, and your stories will live on and impact others. We feel honored to call you our friends.

To our coworkers, friends, and family members who became editors along the way, Peggy Blakley, Susan RyHerd, Nikki Payne, Jacob Payne, TyLinda Blackstock, Donna Lomelino, Sarah Logan, Myrna Lynn, Brenda Hamilton, Norman McCormick, Caleb Payne, Bethany Payne, and Isaac Payne, we are thankful you. Our finished manuscript is a testament to your contributions of time, encouragement, and constructive input.

To Jim and Tonya Folsom and the Folsom family, thank you for the use of your guest house as a writing retreat center. Your hospitality and generosity came at the perfect time. We truly appreciate your servant-heart attitude, and all the ways you have blessed Inner City Mission, as well as our family through the years.

To South Side Christian Church in Springfield, Illinois, and to Lincoln Christian Church in Lincoln, Illinois, thank you for your supportive roles in *Unlocking a Broken World*. You welcomed our family and our residents of Inner City Mission into your spaces and your lives. May God bless your ministries as you continue to usher in life-changing events with grace and mercy.

To our heavenly Father, the Alpha and the Omega, we praise you and thank you for teaching us what we needed to learn most in a broken world. You are the reason and purpose behind every good thing. May the world see you in these pages and glorify your holy name.

# CONTENTS

# PROLOGUE

I watched the little boy squat in the dirt and pick up a few grains of rice. Halting my work, I sat in silence, captivated. This world, unlike any I had confronted before, required mental and emotional processing. The starvation, filth, and disease of the Dominican Republic forced upon me the existence of a parallel world.

I felt moved beyond words at my young age of nineteen.

Before that moment, I had only viewed life from a reclining seat of blessing. My childhood—filled with family, church, and school—had allowed me to stretch out and flourish, making it easy for me to become an admired leader, an oversized fish in my small pond of life.

But everything changed for me that day, sitting on the back of a feed truck. Wedged between two 100-pound sacks of rice, I stopped my bagging to watch the young boy search for his scant morsels. Taking his time, scratching in the dirt, he picked up his grains, one by one, now littered across the dusty plain. His rice had trickled through a tiny hole in his small bag.

My eyes filled with tears. The hole, so minuscule, threatened to steal the only meal his family would have that day. In that short moment, my life stood still.

My world no longer looked the same.

Years later, I would find another world, just as unfamiliar, but closer in proximity. It had existed all around mine, brushing up against my sphere of reality every day, yet never entering. Full of tragic stories, broken people, and chaos, it, too, would pull at the heartstrings of my existence.

Only this time, I had my wife and our children with me.

Looking back now, I can see how my sheltered upbringing and youthful pride worked together to cast a veil of naivety over my eyes, for I entered this world thinking it less-than-worthy of my abilities.

To my surprise and wonderment, I would discover clarity far beyond my furthest expectations. Only God, in his goodness, could lead us to such a place as this, humbling my puffed-up heart.

Come with us if you would into a world that pushed us past ourselves; past our clichés and pat answers, and deeper into truth. The people you meet along the way are real. Their lives and the questions they ask, hard to forget.

Homelessness is merely the backdrop here. The real stage is the ground beneath our feet, where human interaction plays itself out.

In writing this, we changed the names and identifying details of the homeless to protect their children, now grown. Using a fictional approach to nonfiction, we reached back more than twenty years to bring you a story based on real people, real events, and real conversations.

So, now, to the best of our ability, we bring you a story of discovery. May you be blessed and inspired as you travel the road with us into the world of homelessness.

Scott & Connie Payne
*Lord, open our eyes, that we may see your goodness even in darkness. In Jesus' name.*

# ONE

───────────────────────────────────────◦○◦─

# Strange New World

I felt her breath on my face and wondered if Elaine knew anything about body space. Her eyes, six inches from mine, seemed awkward, yet didn't ruffle me. I'd had others unleash their hostility before, hoping to change my mind, but this time surprised me.

A moment earlier, Elaine had sat on the couch relaxed, nodding and smiling. Now she was leaning across my desk, glaring, her hands planted on my paperwork.

"Okay," I said calmly, "you don't have to follow our curfew. But if you don't, it's simple. You cannot stay here. It's your choice, Elaine. What do you want to do?"

Silence wedged between us as she weighed her options. Moments like this are pivotal and allow us to see the real person behind the presentation.

My wife, Connie, was sitting on the edge of the loveseat, watching.

I managed not to jump when Elaine bolted upright, announcing, "Well, then, I'm leaving. I can't stay in a place that won't respect me." Whirling around, she snatched her belongings from the couch and stomped out of the office in an over-the-top, exaggerated sort of way. "No one tells me when to come in at night," she spewed, outraged. "I'm not about to let you start now."

1

Seconds later she charged back in, rescuing her abandoned suitcase from the corner. Dragging it out, she slammed the office door behind her—an end to our apparent absurdity.

"What just happened?" Connie asked, wide-eyed.

"I wish I knew."

Elaine's reaction shocked both of us. Why would something like a curfew be a deal-breaker for someone needing shelter?

We had been working at the mission for three and a half years, yet we still found ourselves with more questions than answers. Every week unveiled a new aspect of homelessness we failed to foresee. Were we just naïve?

Connie and I had both grown up in small farming communities in central Illinois. Miles of cornfield surrounded our childhoods, insulating us, keeping our lives simple, safe.

When we got married, we thought we had all the answers. With a faith to follow God's leading, we tackled life with great expectation. Our first thirteen years produced four of our six children, two successful ministries, and a desire for a new challenge. Then divine providence led us to Inner City Mission, a homeless shelter in Springfield, Illinois, for children, their parents, and single women.

I have to admit, homeless work wasn't in our life plan. Before coming to the mission, I had accepted my dream job with a church-planting organization, only to resign a few months later. God made it clear he had a different plan for our lives.

Not long after, a friend on the board of Inner City Mission asked if I would consider working with the homeless. "A full time position just opened up there," he said with enthusiasm. "Why don't you stop by and see what you think?"

Three days later, we did. While visiting, Connie and I felt God's spirit tugging at us, telling us this is the place. After praying and talking about it for several days, Connie confirmed my own thoughts by saying, "How can we walk away? It feels right—like we're home."

In truth, homeless ministry lay buried at the bottom of things I wanted to do in life. I remember telling God at eighteen, "I'll go anywhere, do anything for you. Just don't send me to a third world country or make me work with the homeless."

Well, God has a sense of humor.

Before accepting my new position, I remember telling Connie, "Don't worry, it's only a bridge to our real ministry—the one God has waiting for us.

"How hard can homeless work be, anyway?" I added. "All we have to do is provide food and shelter while they find a job and save money. After that, they find housing. Move out. Problem solved."

Except homelessness didn't turn out that easy.

After Elaine's dramatic exit, Connie and I sat for a few seconds pondering this strange world of poverty and homelessness. She jumped up, watching Elaine through the window. I heard her say quietly, "Lord, help Elaine find your peace."

I stayed at the desk replaying the events of the past hour.

When Elaine first arrived, I never would have guessed she'd stomp out like that. The woman on the other side of our front door appeared lighthearted, fun. With red sunglasses, a floppy hat, and a flowery bag over one arm, she radiated a beautiful smile.

"I'm Elaine," she told me, presenting her hand. "Do you have any openings?"

Until then, our day had been slow. Connie had brought our two year old son, Jacob, and they were in the back room restocking the supply closet. I had stationed myself at the desk working on a spreadsheet for the next board meeting. I could hear them talking and laughing, sorting through combs and toothbrushes, placing them in cubbyholes.

When the doorbell rang, I called out, "I'll answer it."

"Great, I'll put Jacob down for his nap."

At that time our mission had two red brick buildings. The bigger one, the lodge, was our shelter for homeless families and single women. The other building held offices for staff and a conference room for our meetings. We also had three garages on the property, a storage shed, and a worn-out Lincoln-era cottage that served as our clothing center.

During my first three years at the mission, I had spent most of my days in the lodge working with homeless residents one-on-one. Then I moved into the executive director position. By the time Elaine arrived that day, I'd been working in my new role for six months managing all aspects of the mission.

Though busier now, I still set aside time for our residents. I wanted to stay involved in their lives as much as possible. During our conversations, the lodge supervisor on duty would sit in the office with us taking notes. Connie, expecting our sixth child now, worked weekly shifts as a lodge supervisor.

After shaking Elaine's hand, I stepped back, opening the door wider.

"Yes, we have a room available," I said. "Come on in. I'm Scott."

"Great. I'm homeless."

Elaine bounded over the threshold with an energy that filled the whole living room. A waft of coffee, cigarettes, and Downy followed her in.

She took off her red sunglasses and surveyed her new surroundings. Our living room furniture—all donated by caring people—hardly resembled a showcase, yet looked inviting. Elaine noticed our wide doorway into the kitchen-dining area, and stepped closer to peek in. The yellow walls, white tables, and café curtains offered a cheery mood.

She turned back with bright eyes. "This place seems all right. When can I move in? I need a room right now. My plan is to stay a couple of days while I get a few things worked out, and then I'll be moving on. My suitcase is out on the porch."

Elaine nodded toward the door, dispatching me to retrieve it.

"Now, slow down," I said, bringing in her suitcase. "We need to discuss a few things and fill out paperwork." I motioned to my left. "Come in here and we'll get started."

"Perfect." She breezed by me into the lodge office where Connie had entered from the back.

Along with storing supplies for residents, the room in the back offered a bed for lodge supervisors during their overnight shifts. We had placed a small cot back there for Jacob.

Elaine headed straight for Connie, shaking her hand. "I'm Elaine. I'll be staying here a few days."

"Glad to meet you," she said, introducing herself. "Feel free to sit on the couch while I get the forms." Opening a file drawer, Connie pulled out an intake packet, laying it on the metal desk.

Elaine plopped on the couch, crossing her legs Indian style. She looked comfortable, as if she'd been here before.

Connie grabbed a clipboard and went to the loveseat, while I rolled my chair into position behind the desk. I opened the intake packet. "Is this your first time here?" Although I hadn't recognized Elaine, I wanted to locate her file in case she'd stayed here before.

"Yes, and just so you know, it wasn't my idea to come." Elaine tossed her hat aside and fluffed out her red-brown curls. "I got in a bind, if you know what I mean." She winked at me as if I'd understand, but I didn't. I figured I'd find out soon enough.

Before anyone moves in, we go through an intake process. We gather personal information, hand out forms, and talk about expectations. None of these things obligate a person or family to stay for any length of time. Each has the freedom to walk away. Yet anyone choosing to stay must agree to our basic living requirements and sign our releases.

"Our main concern above everything else," I told her, "is to maintain a safe environment for everyone living, working, or visiting here."

"Sounds good to me," she said, with a spirited nod.

"Let me explain how our shelter works. We will assign daily chores for you and add your name to our supper rotation. That means you get to cook one night a week. If you don't know how to cook, someone will help you learn."

"Oh, I love cooking."

"That's great. We need enthusiastic cooks around here. Maybe you'll inspire the others."

"Well, I've had plenty of experience. All my jobs center around food it seems. Let's see, I've waitressed, cooked, decorated cakes. Even catered before."

"Wonderful. You should fit in great here."

Her upbeat attitude amazed me. It's not often that a happy homeless person shows up on our doorstep.

"Now, along with chores, you'll be responsible for cleaning your room and washing your own clothes. We have a laundry room downstairs and a washing schedule on the wall behind you. Feel free to sign up in an open timeslot."

"We have detergent in the back room if you need it," Connie offered. "We don't always have dryer sheets."

"I'll give you a key to your room," I said, "and the combination to one of these lockers against the wall."

Elaine's eyes took in our metal lockers with red, chipping paint, relics from a local grade school.

"We cannot be responsible for lost or stolen items, so please lock up anything valuable. If you have any medicines, you'll need to store them here for everyone's safety."

She nodded, fluffing her curls again.

"And if you smoke, you'll have to go outside, away from the doors. We have a deck out back where you can relax and visit with others."

"I wish I didn't," she said, reaching into her bag. She pulled out a big pack of gum and held it up with a sheepish smile. "I've quit more times than I can remember."

Connie glanced up from taking notes. "Everyone says it's hard. Prayer really helps."

Elaine rolled her eyes. "Well, I've tried everything else. Wouldn't hurt, I guess."

We spent the next fifteen minutes going through the house rules.

Eager and attentive, Elaine seemed ready to plunge into shelter life. Most people hit low points in their lives before coming to us, making it clear they don't want to be here. But with Elaine, everything appeared pleasant, almost too painless.

"Now, before you sign our intake forms, let me explain our evening curfew."

Elaine sat upright, raising an eyebrow.

"Monday through Thursday, you must be here on mission property by five o'clock. On weekends, it's seven."

Her jaw dropped. I know I didn't say solitary confinement, but the look on her face said otherwise. She uncrossed her legs, dropping both feet to the floor.

I tried to soften the blow. "You can get a pass to stay out later if—"

Elaine sprang from the couch to my desk. That's when I felt her breath.

"No one imposes a curfew on my life *ever*," she said, through clenched teeth.

Thinking about our conversation now, after her abrupt

departure, I wouldn't change anything I'd said. If I had lifted the curfew like she wanted, to pacify her, I would have set the stage for greater confrontations in the future.

In her mind, *all* boundaries would be movable.

Elaine came to us needing shelter. A priority in her life, we assumed. Yet her demand for freedom—to come and go as she pleased—trumped having a place to eat and sleep.

She wanted things done her way, on her terms.

And we had to let her walk out.

# TWO

## The Sidewalk

"I can't believe she's leaving," Connie said, leaning on the window sill. "It doesn't make sense."

I stood and looked out the window. Elaine, halfway down our front sidewalk, marched with great flair, her suitcase skipping behind on rickety wheels.

"I wonder if Elaine always stomps off when she doesn't get her way," I said. "She reminds me of that insanity quote, 'Doing the same thing over and over, but expecting a different result.'"[1]

"Yeah, I don't get it."

Seating myself, I tried to clear my mind and focus on my spreadsheet. It's never easy watching people make poor decisions.

Connie moved to a different window.

"That's strange," she said. "Elaine stopped at the end of the sidewalk and she's talking, but I don't see anyone out there with her."

I rose halfway and looked. Sure enough, Elaine was outside alone, waving her hands, and talking. "Keep an eye on her and let me know if anything changes. She may be harmless, but we're responsible for a house full of people."

I returned to my spreadsheet.

A minute or so passed.

9

"Now she's looking around, searching the landscape," Connie said. "Maybe she's waiting on someone. "Lord, bring her back if we can help her."

Connie stepped closer to the window.

"Well, now she's pacing circles around her suitcase, talking to herself again."

At least she's outside, I thought, weighing the idea of going out to check on her.

"Wait, she's facing the mission," Connie said, getting excited. "I think she's coming back."

Surprised, I stood again. We watched Elaine take a few halting steps toward the front porch. Pausing, she glanced around, and then continued. At the porch, she lifted her suitcase over the three steps, climbing them, and she disappeared from our view.

Connie and I looked at each other. We heard nothing.

"Do you think she wants to stay?"

I shrugged. "I hope so. I'd like to help her if we can."

We didn't know if Elaine would ring the doorbell, knock, or leave, so we waited.

Then we heard her light knock.

I opened the front door. Elaine, gazing up at me, had her head tilted like a puppy wanting forgiveness. "Can I try this one more time?"

Before I could answer, she stuck out her hand and spoke in a high, chipper voice. "Hi, my name is Elaine and I am homeless. Do you have any openings?"

I had to smile. I wasn't convinced the woman was sane, but she showed creativity and resolve.

"As a matter of fact, we do," I said, shaking her hand, "and we still have a curfew. Will that be a problem?" I stood in the doorway, not budging. We had to be clear on this.

"No, it won't be a problem at all. I don't plan on being here long enough for it to matter. I'm getting a job and moving on."

"In that case, come on in." I stepped aside. "You still have to sign our intake forms before you can move in."

I followed her into the office where Connie greeted her.

"Welcome back, Elaine. I'm glad you changed your mind."

"Me, too," she said in a flat voice. She parked her suitcase by the couch before sitting.

I went to the desk. "So why did you come back? What changed your mind?

"I don't want to talk about it." She rummaged through her bag for tissues.

"We talk about everything here. Nothing's off the table. You might as well be honest with yourself and the rest of us. Why did you come back?"

"Wow, you get straight to the point."

"I usually do." I settled back in my chair. I had plenty of time. If Elaine wanted our help, she would have to open up.

Blotting a tear, she sighed.

"When I got to the end of the sidewalk, I realized I have nowhere to go. I'm thirty-eight years old, and I've lived in this area my whole life. I know hundreds of people around here. People I went to grade school with, and high school. People I've worked with through the years. I even have relatives living nearby. But I realized for the first time, I have no one in my life who would take me in."

Tears rolled down her face.

"I have no place to go. When I got to the end of the sidewalk, I froze. I didn't know which way to turn. Out of all those people, there wasn't *one* person I could call for a ride.

"Dozens of faces flashed through my mind. But I knew no one would come. It was the worst feeling ever. I felt totally alone."

She wiped her tears.

"How did my life come to this? I've broken everyone's trust. When I was out on the sidewalk, I asked myself, 'Can this be true? Am I completely, utterly alone?'

"The answer I got back was 'yes,' and it stabbed me right here."

Elaine thumped her heart.

"I felt pain, real pain. Not just my own, but the pain I've caused my family and friends. I've hurt so many people. Especially the ones I love most, like my daughters—."

She dropped her head, sobbing.

Laying her notes aside, Connie joined her on the couch. I rolled my chair around to the front of the desk. We waited for her tears to subside.

"I've hurt my daughters, both of my beautiful girls," she said, blowing into tissues. "They want me gone from their lives."

"Is their father in the picture?" I asked gently.

"My girls have different fathers, and neither wants me around. The truth is, my exes want nothing to do with me. I've hurt 'em too many times. I don't know what's wrong with me."

Her red-rimmed eyes turned to Connie.

"When you mentioned prayer earlier, I'd forgotten all about God. I used to pray when I was a little girl to feel better, but it's been years. Outside, I tried praying again. I know this sounds stupid, but I said, 'God, if you're really there, can you help me out? I'm in such a mess. I have nowhere to go.'

"Honestly, I didn't expect to hear anything. God never answered my prayers before. But this time, I heard a quiet voice in my head say, *'Elaine, you always do things your way. You live for yourself and take what you want. Look at where you are now. Every decision in your life has led you to this place.'*

"Well, that shook me, and got me thinking about my life.

Actually, I started talking out loud. My brain felt overloaded. For the first time, I saw every bad decision and every person I ever hurt in my life."

She pulled out another tissue.

"Why couldn't I see this before?" She searched our faces for an answer.

"Then I started thinking, if every decision I made was bad and led me to this place, then I must be making the wrong decision now by leaving. Maybe I should stay here and listen to these people. I don't want anyone telling me what to do—or when to come in at night—but maybe that's what I need.

"After that, I felt calm. I knew I had to stay. But then I remembered how obnoxious I acted earlier and hated the idea of facing you again. I didn't think you'd give me another chance."

"That's what we're here for," Connie said, with a reassuring nod.

Elaine patted her face dry.

"Coming back scares me, but I really *do* want things to be different. I don't want to keep hurting people. I can't let my daughters down again. The last thing I want to do is go back to my old life. But it's all I know. As a young girl, I acted stingy and selfish and always demanded everyone's attention."

Her eyes filled.

"What if I can't change? Maybe this is who I am."

"It doesn't have to be that way," I said. "Most people can change with the right help."

She perked up a bit, sitting straighter.

"As I walked back to the shelter, I told myself, 'I won't be here long. I'll find a job, save money, and get back in the game before the end of the month.' I kept repeating this until you opened the door."

She looked around the room.

"So here I am, sitting in a homeless shelter. I'm embarrassed, but I *am* grateful. I promise I won't stay long. I'm saving every penny and getting a place of my own. You'll see."

Her tears ran down.

"I'm going to work hard and make everyone proud of me."

Hearing that, I felt certain things would get better for her. Yes, she created pain and disappointment in her life, but at least she was on the right track now. Honesty with oneself is the first step toward taking responsibility.

"Thank you for trusting us," Connie said. "Do you mind if I pray with you?"

"I need all the prayers I can get."

Her words were simple. "Lord, help Elaine find the joy and peace she longs for. In Jesus' name."

"Do you really think I can find peace in my life? And joy?"

"I do," I answered. "With God's love, you can find a relationship in Jesus Christ that will change your life forever."

"That stuff scares me. It doesn't make any sense."

"Don't worry about it now. Let's finish your paperwork and get you to your room."

Elaine signed our forms—including the curfew agreement—and followed Connie upstairs to her new room: a small, private bedroom, about ten-by-twelve, with a closet, a set of bunk beds, a chest of drawers, and a lamp.

Nothing fancy, but Elaine moved in that day and made herself at home.

# THREE

## Fast Track

Two days after her arrival, Elaine rushed into the office with an announcement, "I have a job!" She spun around squealing, waving her hands in the air.

I gave her a high five. "Congratulations. I believe you set the record. Where will you be working?"

"Monte's Grill, downtown. They just opened last month. I'll be waiting tables at first, but I hope to run the grill later." She let out another squeal.

"You were smart finding a job within walking distance from here. When do you start?"

"Tomorrow. The manager said if I do well in training the next couple of days, I can start waiting tables on my own Friday night." Twirling, she danced a little jig. "Since I have a lot of experience, I think I can handle it."

Her good news confirmed what Connie and I had thought from the beginning. If we give the homeless a helping hand—food and a place to stay—they can find jobs, save money, and get back on their feet.

Elaine's bliss calmed down and she slowed to a stop in front of me. "If my training goes well, I'll need to work late Friday night. If I have to clean up, it may be midnight."

"That's fine. Connie's scheduled for the Friday overnight. I'll be here with her and let you in."

Elaine hooted, prancing toward the doorway. She circled back. "Hey, Scott, can I call my daughter?"

"Sure." I pressed a button on the office telephone. "Line one is yours." She made a dash to the living room phone. Within seconds, the whole lodge heard her exciting news.

Elaine tackled her job training with energy and zeal, impressing both her manager and direct supervisor. On Thursday, they agreed she could wait tables on her own Friday night.

All of us were thrilled for her. Homelessness would only be a bump in the road for Elaine. Her success made us believe anyone could move forward in life with a little help and motivation.

Before leaving for work on Friday, Elaine came into the lodge office for a pass. She had to sign our slip of paper allowing her to stay out past curfew. I wrote down one o'clock as her return time, giving her leeway for walking back. I felt comfortable letting her stay out longer. Her new job was a major step toward independence.

After signing the pass, Elaine whooped a few times, waving her crisp apron in the air. We all clapped and cheered as she left the building, joining in her moment of triumph. Elaine, a full-fledged waitress, was about to start her first real shift. We believed she was on the fast track, about to find success.

We said a quick prayer for her, and focused our attention on other residents in the lodge. Being busy, we didn't think about Elaine again for several hours.

Although Connie was the official lodge supervisor on duty, I would often come with her for the overnights. We'd bring our children and work together as a family unit.

At the mission our kids learned compassion, tough love, and how to deal with chaos. On the flip side, the residents observed our family, how we interacted, and how Connie and I parented. The mutual benefits outweighed any concerns we had at first, and to this day our grown children thank us for the wide spectrum of experiences they gained at the mission.

The lodge housed an average of twenty-five people a night. We would later remodel rooms in our office building next door to accommodate more residents, but at this time we offered twelve rooms, and they stayed full most of the time.

After settling our children into bed for the night, Connie joined me in the living room with several of our mothers. Some of our best conversations took place in the evening in the peaceful aftermath of sleeping children. I knew my wife looked forward to this time.

Yet, within the hour, she looked exhausted. Connie always wanted to do more, give more, but taking care of five children—with our sixth on the way—took most of her energy. I encouraged her to go to bed.

When she left, I returned to the office and finished logging the day's events into the computer. Each day we would document conversations, situations, and changes taking place in the lodge. This would allow the next supervisor on duty to catch up on recent happenings.

I glanced at the clock. Eleven-thirty. The lodge living room had quieted, with most people retiring to their rooms. I wondered about Elaine's first night on the job, assuming she wouldn't arrive until midnight. I looked forward to hearing about her evening.

In her short time here, Elaine had turned her life around. She'd found a decent-paying job, had started making new friends, and was already planning for her future. That excited me. After a conversation or two about taking responsibility, Elaine had surged forward with new motivation and hope.

"Coming here gave me a fresh start," she'd told us that morning. "Now I'm ready to jump in and tackle life again."

Thinking about her success gave me an idea.

I could use her story in our expansion plans for the mission. At our last three board meetings, we had talked about ways to enlarge our facilities, to increase the number of people we could work with at any given time. Raising money for this might be easier if we could share Elaine's success with our donors.

Expanding our services seemed like the logical next step. Connie and I believed we had solutions, and we hoped to have a greater impact on the homeless population in central Illinois.

In reality, I don't suppose we had many answers at this point, but we truly desired to help more people. Deep down, I have to admit, I had another reason for wanting to expand. Our shelter was small compared to other rescue missions across the country, and that embarrassed me at times. I wanted to work with hundreds of homeless instead of the twenty-five we averaged daily. Like many in ministry today, I had bought into the idea that bigger is better.

In my earlier ministries, God had blessed me with wonderful opportunities to make a difference. I faced life-sized issues involving large sums of money and thrived on the challenges. It thrilled me to be used by God as an instrument of change.

But now, doing inner city homeless work in a limited, cramped space was tough, and to be honest, a blow to my ego. Wouldn't our ministry—and me, for that matter—be more significant if we could expand our reach?

I shut down the computer and looked at the clock. Midnight. Elaine would be showing up soon. Time slows when you're waiting, so I picked up the newspaper and looked through want ads. Maybe I could find a job prospect for someone.

Before long, the want ads led to the sports page. Then to the comics. One o'clock came, and then one-thirty. I ended up reading the whole newspaper. Where was Elaine? I hoped she hadn't run into trouble. Surely she'd let us know she had an emergency.

At two-thirty I turned out the lights and went to bed. Whatever happened, I hoped Elaine was okay.

*Lord, protect her and bring her back safe.*

Around eight o'clock that morning, I made a round through the lodge. I wanted to make sure everyone was up and moving for the day. I checked Elaine's room first, hoping someone had let her in.

No one had.

In the kitchen I offered to help the ladies with breakfast. "We just poured our last batch of pancakes on the griddle," Connie said. "You can let everyone know we're ready." That day we had thirteen adults and fourteen children in the house, plus our family of seven, which meant lots of pancakes. I saw several stacks on the counter ready to go.

After breakfast, Connie gathered our children and left for piano lessons since her shift ended at nine. I settled in for the day, having agreed to cover for our next lodge supervisor until five. I wanted to stay anyway to find out about Elaine.

I walked into the living room and turned on cartoons for the kids. A chorus of, "Thank you, Mr. Payne," echoed from children plopping on the floor behind me.

"You're welcome," I said, patting several heads on my way through. I thought about their young lives, all they'd experienced. Children are truly the innocent ones in the homeless world.

My thoughts changed when the back door opened. I pivoted toward the kitchen and saw a woman entering the lodge.

Haggard, yet recognizable, she kept her head down and rushed toward me into the living room. Glancing up, spotting me, she froze. Then she bolted for the stairs.

My mouth fell open. Until that instant, I still carried hope Elaine had good reason for not coming back. Now I could see she was stoned and coming off some kind of high. Her bloodshot eyes and matted hair let me know it was an all-night marathon.

I felt stunned and let down.

I didn't follow her. I had to process what I saw.

Trudging back to the office, I sank into my chair, numb. In that moment I had to face the truth: I had no real understanding of homelessness.

Sitting in the quiet, I pondered my realization.

Why did I think Elaine would be our picture of success? What made me believe she would pave the way for others, inspire them to leap into their future as she had?

*How could I be so wrong, God? What did I miss?*

I leaned back in my chair, watching a squirrel climb a tree outside the window.

*Lord, why didn't I see this?*

A gentle thought offered an answer.

*You care more about your plans for expansion than you do about Elaine. You're so busy trying to expand "your" kingdom, you couldn't see into her world.*

That wasn't true. Or was it? I wanted to defend myself, tell God I cared about Elaine more. But at that moment, I knew the truth. At some point, I'd gotten sidetracked. My desire for significance had risen higher than Elaine. That shocked me. I'd always tried to be pure in heart. Yet my dreams to expand *my* ministry, *my* kingdom, made it impossible for me to have a pure heart or a clear mind.

In the midst of my self-sightedness, I had missed the signs.

When Elaine admitted to us she partied, she never mentioned her drug use. I failed to ask.

When Elaine said she'd broken everyone's trust, I didn't bother to find out why. I wanted to believe she'd turned a corner. All things were new.

Whenever one of us brought up faith, she said the "whole Christian thing" wasn't for her. It may work for others, she allowed, but not for her. Finding a job and moving out was far more important. She wanted to make homelessness a distant memory. We cheered her on, assuming she could.

In truth, I let her down. In my selfish ambition, I clung to the idea that providing food and shelter was the answer to homelessness. I wanted to believe everything would fall into place once a person finds a job and saves money. It made perfect sense in *my* world. Giving folks a helping hand in their time of need would move them forward, let them carry on.

Not in this world.

*Father, forgive my selfish pride, my blind ignorance. Show me how to help Elaine. Teach me how to expand YOUR kingdom, not mine.*

I mulled over Elaine's condition for the rest of the morning, praying for direction and insight. No matter what, I didn't want her to self-destruct. Kicking her out on the street didn't make sense.

I reached for a bible, turning to Matthew 6:33. "But seek first his kingdom and his righteousness, and all these things will be added to you."[1]

*What do you mean by this, Lord?*

Flipping through Romans, I read the Apostle Paul's words in chapter 14 verse 17, "For the kingdom of God is…righteousness, peace and joy in the Holy Spirit."[2]

*God, how does that work in the homeless world? In Elaine's world?*

I reflected on these scriptures, praying for clarity. I could see Paul wasn't talking about the physical expansion of God's kingdom. Rather, he spoke of God's supernatural expansion of righteousness, peace, and joy found in the Holy Spirit.

*How can we help Elaine find this?*

Contemplating, I got an idea. Instead of kicking her out, maybe we should set up a hedge of protection around her. Elaine needed intervention, not rejection. Even more, she needed to experience the kingdom of God around her. Maybe then she could embrace his joy and peace for herself.

But would she be willing?

I'd have to find out.

# FOUR

## A Pocket Full of Change

After lunch I went upstairs and knocked on Elaine's door. I could hear her deep rhythmic breathing. I knocked louder.

"Elaine, wake up. We need to talk."

A slow, groggy voice answered. "Okay, I'm getting up. Give me ten minutes."

"Take your time. Just come down to the office when you can."

Forty-five minutes later, Elaine made it downstairs. She slumped against the office doorway, silent. Her flowery bag and suitcase lay at her feet. I motioned for her to come in, but she didn't move. Instead, she looked away, speaking in monotone. "I started using last night and couldn't stop. I know you want me out, so I'm leaving."

"What makes you so sure I'm kicking you out?"

She glanced at me, wary.

"Come into the office." I waved for her to come in.

Elaine hung back a few seconds, then clumped in, leaving her belongings at the door. Without a shred of her usual vitality, she dropped onto the couch.

"So what happened last night?"

She inhaled deeply, staring at the floor.

"I arrived at work and everything went great. People seemed

23

happy with my service. Everyone enjoyed their meals. I've worked at jobs like this before and learned a long time ago how to make people happy. Waiting tables makes me feel alive. In control. Like I'm the center of attention."

She lifted her eyes, waiting for my reaction. I just nodded.

"What surprised me most was the money. I've never gotten tips like that before. It really amazed me, with Monte's being a new restaurant and all. I didn't expect to earn that much. But my pockets overflowed. It felt good, like I did something right. I don't remember the last time I felt that good.

"Afterward, my boss said I did a fantastic job. I clocked out at midnight totally exhausted, but on cloud nine. I slipped out the back door hoping no one would see me. All I wanted was a hot shower and a good night's sleep.

"I walked across the parking lot thinking about my evening: the customers, the rush to get hot food to the tables, and the bazillion rolls I served. My night just flew by. And I made no big blunders, which was surprising. I felt so proud of myself, like I had performed a great feat."

"Then, before I even got off the property, my thoughts changed. I began hearing terrible things. That always happen when I do something right. Voices pester me and make me feel awful.

"Last night, they said, '*Sure, you made good money, but you'll never keep it up. You can't focus on anything long enough to be successful. What makes you think you're good enough now? You always let people down.*'"

Tears streamed down her face. I handed her the tissue box.

"The voices kept getting louder and meaner, making me feel worse with every step. They laughed at me, saying, '*No wonder your friends and family deserted you. They know the real truth. You're a fraud, and you'll always be a fraud.*'

"Hearing that, I reached into my pockets and held onto my dollars and coins, hoping my tips would calm me. Instead, I panicked."

She rubbed tears away with a tissue.

"Please believe me when I say I didn't plan on using. I didn't even think about it until I heard these words, *'Your anxieties can be gone in an instant. Every thought will disappear.'*

"I tried to fight back. I even yelled, 'Wait, I've been clean for a week. I have everything under control. My new job is great and I'm doing well.'

"That's when I heard people coming out of the restaurant behind me. I wish I'd kept on walking, but I turned around and saw three of my co-workers laughing and having a good time. They waved at me to join them. I knew where they were going. I heard 'em talking about a party earlier.

"I didn't move...I couldn't decide what to do. Then a nicer, gentler voice said, *'One line would be okay, just enough to get you through the night. You deserve it. You worked hard and made good money tonight. Your new friends will see how strong you are, and how you can stop anytime you want.'*

"Inside, I knew it wasn't right, but I didn't have the energy to fight. I thought about the party and all the people I would meet. My heart started pounding. I knew the decision was made.

"I walked over to join them, to join the fun...like I always seem to do."

Tears spilled down her cheeks.

"I just wanted to drown out the voices and feel better. I started with a simple line of coke. That's all I planned on doing. But when they offered me another, and another, I couldn't stop.

She sighed.

"Sunrise came and my pockets were empty. My whole night, wasted."

Elaine stifled a sob with her tissues. "I feel so ashamed."

Her sadness and disappointment felt heavy on my heart.

"I have all my stuff right there." She nodded toward the doorway. "I plan on leaving."

Seeing her red, puffy eyes, I rolled my chair back. "Stay here. I'll be right back."

I found a washcloth in our small bathroom in the back, and soaked it in cold water.

*Lord, what do you want me to do?*

Wringing out the cloth, I recognized the only real option I had. Elaine needed a hedge of protection. Like most shelters, we don't tolerate drug use. In fact, we tell people up front if they use, they'll be asked to leave. By letting Elaine stay, I'd be going against our own policy. Yet nothing else made sense.

A peace came over me, and I returned to the office. I handed the wet cloth to Elaine. She covered her face with it, laying her head back on the couch.

I returned to the desk.

"Well, I've prayed and pondered over your situation for several hours, and I've made a decision."

Elaine bolted upright, dropping the cloth on her lap.

"I want you to stay. I believe you need another chance. I feel partly responsible for what happened last night."

She stared at me, dumbfounded.

"When you told us you partied, I didn't ask you a single question about that part of your life. I wanted to believe your new job would solve your homelessness. In fact, I planned for you to be the face of the mission. I wanted to use your success story to inspire people to give money, so we could expand our facilities.

"I'm really sorry. I should have done my job better."

Her eyes opened wider.

"I hope you can forgive me."

26

She stared at me for a few seconds.

"I don't get it," she said. "I stayed out all night spending my tip money on drugs. I came back wasted. And *you're* apologizing to me?"

"Yeah, I suppose it seems strange, but in these past few hours, I discovered something about myself I really don't like. And I have you to thank for that."

Elaine pressed the cloth against her face.

"I don't get it at all," she said through her wet rag. "But I'm glad you're letting me stay. I have nowhere else to go. I thought for sure you were putting me out. That's what they do in rehab centers. I should know. I'm the queen of rehab in central Illinois."

She cast the cloth aside.

"If I had to leave right now, I know I would die out there on the street. I can't stop doing this stuff. I have ghosts haunting me or something. I need help."

Tears flooded her eyes.

"We can deal with that later," I said. "First, I need to clarify a few things. If you stay, I'll need to put you on complete house restriction for at least six weeks. You'll go nowhere and see no one. That means no job either."

I paused, letting my words sink in. I wanted to give her a chance to stomp out.

She didn't flinch.

"While you're on house restriction, plan to attend church. We don't force people to go, but in your case—because of your addictions—I want you to be supervised at all times. Be ready to board the van with our lodge supervisor at nine o'clock on Sunday mornings."

Elaine offered her first smile of the day. "Okay, maybe church will be good for me. I'll try to keep an open mind."

"And plan on talking with us about your life, every aspect.

We can't help you unless we know what's going on with you. We don't have all the answers, but for now, you'll be assigned extra chores, more mentoring classes, and a few reading assignments. I want you to learn how to make positive changes in your life. Are you willing to do these things?"

"I'll do whatever it takes to change my life."

Rallying a bit of energy, she sat up straighter.

"I never told you why I came to the mission. I felt too ashamed. But you may as well know the truth. The day I arrived here, my daughter, Carrie, drove me. The night before, I showed up at her house high as a kite and drunk. I walked through her front door and threw up all over her living room carpet. Then I passed out. I hate to say it, but it wasn't the first time.

"The next day after sleeping it off, Carrie asked me to ride with her to the grocery store. I agreed, thinking all was forgotten. Well, instead of going to the store, she drove me here. She parked the car out front and said, 'Mom, don't come back to our house again. My son isn't growing up around your mess the way I had to. Your suitcase is on the floor in the backseat.'

"I sat there, dazed. I couldn't believe it. Carrie reached across and opened my door and said, 'Get out, Mom. If any place can help you, this one can.'

"I felt my heart ripping apart. I begged her to give me one more chance. But she wouldn't."

Elaine picked up the cloth again, patting her eyes.

"It's just as well, I guess. I would have hurt her again. I honestly believed I could beat the drugs and the booze. I always hoped things would get better…but they only got worse."

She laid her head back, closing her eyes.

"Sometimes it takes losing everything," I said, "before you can admit you need help. Your life may feel hopeless right now, but I believe you're at a place of humility. The Bible talks about this as being poor in spirit,[1] which isn't a bad place to be. Maybe now, God can begin the process of healing your life. If you're willing."

Elaine lifted her head, curious. I knew this was new for her.

"It won't happen overnight. My dad used to tell me, 'Son, it takes time to carve steps into the side of that hole you've dug yourself in.' And he's right. But know this: God will help you if you let him."

She moved forward to the edge of the couch. "I want to give God a chance this time, I really do. I'm ready to let someone help me for once. Heaven knows, I've tried everything else."

"Take advantage of your time here. God will give you a whole new life if you want it."

Elaine, pondering my words, brought the cloth to the desk and walked to the doorway.

"I'll tell you up front," she said, reaching down for her bags, "I don't know what that means or how it works, but if you're willing to show me, I'll try."

# FIVE

## Born Homeless

Elaine settled into the mission with a whole new mindset. She knew she needed to be here and looked upon each day as an opportunity for growth. In the process, she pushed our parameters and stretched our thinking in a way only God could orchestrate.

She wasn't the only one. Others would come, affecting us in profound ways. Each person, uniquely broken, had a common need for healing. More than once, Connie and I felt our hearts breaking in the face of a person's tragic circumstances.

One week into Elaine's house restriction, I opened the front door of the lodge to retrieve the morning newspaper. Bending down, I saw in front of me a pair of saturated shoes in a thin puddle of water. Startled, I dropped the newspaper and stepped back. A young woman soaked head-to-toe stood on our front porch.

*Did she stay out all night in the rain?* I wondered. I still felt a spring mist in the air.

"My name is Heidi," she said in a soft voice. "Do you have any rooms?"

Her chin quivered.

"Yes, we do. Come on in. I'm Scott." Heidi slogged into the living room, being careful to stay on the welcome mat. She rubbed her arms to get warm.

Elaine vaulted herself from an overstuffed chair. "I'll bring towels."

"That would be great," I said.

Heidi turned toward me. "Thank you for inviting me in." Her smile intensified a deep sadness in her eyes.

"You're welcome. We had a room open up last night, but let's talk about that after you dry off and get warm."

She shivered, and droplets of water trickled down her forehead.

Elaine brought towels as Shelly, our lodge supervisor on duty, entered the kitchen from the downstairs pantry. Seeing Heidi's condition, she dumped her box of canned goods on a table and rushed into the living room. She snatched two towels from Elaine's pile, draping them around her.

"You have perfect timing," I said to Shelly. "Can you take Heidi next door to Miss Daisy's and help her find a dry outfit?"

Miss Daisy, our beloved volunteer of many years, ran our clothing center full-time. A World War II widow in her late sixties, she never bothered to remarry or learn how to drive. She often slept in our old green cottage on the property whenever it rained or snowed. All of us at the mission had become her family.

"Sure, no problem," Shelly said.

Elaine stepped forward, wrapping an arm around Heidi's shoulders. "I want to go, too, if that's okay." She looked like a protective older sister.

"That's fine. When you ladies come back, bring Heidi to the office and we'll talk."

I watched them exit through the back door, and couldn't help but wonder why a young woman had stayed out all night in the rain. I felt sad for her, yet puzzled.

*Doesn't she have family or friends to fall back on?*

Twenty minutes later, the ladies came back, chattering like old friends. Heidi seemed more at ease now, especially around Elaine. I invited them into the office.

"Did you meet Miss Daisy?" I asked her.

Tears formed in Heidi's eyes. "She remembered my name and gave me a hug like I was her granddaughter. She didn't care if I dripped on her floor."

"Miss Daisy is a special lady. She'll take you under her wing if you let her."

I reached into a file drawer and took out an intake packet. "Do you mind if Elaine joins us?"

"I'd like that." She gave Elaine a shy smile.

I invited Heidi and Elaine to sit on the couch and offered the desk to Shelly since she preferred taking notes on the computer. I moved to the loveseat with the packet.

I glanced over at Heidi. Her slight build and pixie haircut made me think of a young school girl. She couldn't weigh much more than a hundred pounds. I wondered how she knew Miss Daisy.

"Have you stayed here before?" I asked, opening the packet.

"Yeah, when I was sixteen. I needed a place to stay while Family Services looked for a foster home for me and my two-month old son."

I laid the packet aside. "Why don't we go through the intake process later? I'd like to check next door to see if we have a record of your stay."

"Okay."

"For now, would you mind telling us why you came to the mission this morning?"

"I don't mind. Where do you want me to start?"

"Well, how about at the beginning? When did you become homeless?"

Heidi looked off in the distance.

She spoke slowly, as if realizing for the first time the impact of her words.

"I was born homeless."

The clarity and honesty of her simple answer grabbed my soul. Somehow, I knew at that moment, I was sitting on the edge of knowledge, about to be schooled on homelessness.

"My birth mom is white and so was her husband," she explained, "but as you can see, I'm mixed—half black, half white." Heidi touched the skin on her arm. "This is why I'm homeless."

Tears hovered on her lower lashes. Elaine grabbed the tissue box, pulling one out for her.

"What do you mean?" I asked. "Were your parents homeless?"

"That's not what I'm saying. You see, right after I was born, my mom's husband took one look at me and knew I wasn't his. He got furious and told her, 'Get rid of that child or you'll never step foot in my house again.'

"I think he really hated me."

"That's terrible," Shelly said, glaring over the keyboard. "It wasn't your fault."

"I'm not sure about that." A tear slid down Heidi's face.

"All I know is my mom decided to get rid of me. Not right away. She got an apartment in Peoria and kept me for a couple of months. Then she drove me back here to Springfield and dropped me off at my bio dad's trailer. Why she did that, I don't know. She knew he was an abusive man with a bad temper. I guess she wanted me gone from her life and he was the quickest, easiest way."

She wiped her cheek.

"My mother showed up at his trailer and dumped me in his arms, saying, 'She's your problem now,' and walked off. Then she went back to her husband. At least that's what my bio dad told me.

"So there I was, all alone in the hands of a mean and disgusting alcoholic. I don't know how I survived. I think his mom and aunt helped out some."

The office phone rang, drawing our attention. Shelly answered the call, and then the doorbell rang. "I'll get it," I said, jumping up. We were used to things happening at once in the lodge. At the front door, I accepted a box of used clothing from an older gentleman and gave him a receipt.

Carrying the box in, I told Heidi, "You'll get used to our interruptions."

She waited patiently for us to finish before continuing.

"I remember hearing my bio dad say I was good for one thing: helping him find girlfriends. I was his ice breaker. A woman would see me, think I was cute, and start asking my dad questions. Before long, we'd move into her place. That happened over and over. I lived out of a bag for years.

"Growing up, I secretly hoped one of my dad's girlfriends would love me and want to be my mom, but that never happened. Dad was too obnoxious and selfish. We never stayed anywhere too long, which was just as well. Most of his girlfriends hated me."

Heidi paused, shivering again. Her hair was still damp.

"Let me find you a blanket," Shelly said, going toward the back room.

"Are you okay?" I asked. "Is this too much right now?"

"Oh, no. It feels good to talk."

Shelly reappeared with a fuzzy blanket, tucking it around her. Thanking her, Heidi resumed her story.

"My father ran a tavern, so I grew up in a bar. My playhouse was the stockroom, and my toys were empty beer bottles and boxes.

"Sometimes I played outside in the gravel parking lot, but mostly I hung around the regulars, the drunks coming to the bar every day. A few were really nice, but others..."

Her voice trailed off.

Elaine handed her another tissue.

"I lived with my father and his pathetic girlfriends for eleven years. I can't say everything was bad. I had teachers who liked me, who thought I was smart. One said I was the best reader in my class. Others tried to give me extra homework and books to read, but Dad always threw them in the dumpster. He said I didn't have time. I had to keep the stockroom clean and dishes washed. I also had errands to run and laundry to do."

Heidi pulled the blanket around tighter.

"After awhile, my teachers stopped sending books home with me. Then one day, Family Services showed up at school. I don't know who made the call, but they made me go to the office and answer a bunch of their questions. They talked to me first, then several others. Afterward, they said I couldn't live with my dad anymore.

"They took me to a foster home to live with a real family. At first I was scared, but my new parents seemed really nice. They gave me my own bedroom, brand new clothes, and lots of toys. I couldn't believe it. For the first time in my life, I had a real family who cared about me. I loved being there."

Tears welled in her eyes.

"It didn't last very long. The foster dad started coming into my bedroom...every morning. I hated waking up...I hated *him*... but I loved my new family.

Her tears began to fall.

"After six months of this, I couldn't take it anymore and started crying hysterically one night. I locked myself in a bedroom and called the police. When my foster parents found out, they threatened to kill themselves. The dad promised he'd jump off the building across the street if I told them anything. The mom ran around the house all crazy, searching for a gun. She kept screaming, 'If you talk, I'll shoot myself and it'll be your fault!'

"That terrified me. I ran outside and hid in the front ditch waiting for the police. I remember being flat on my back in the pitch dark, crying, listening to locusts. They chirped so loud that night."

More tears trickled down.

"I can't stand locusts now. They make me sick to my stomach.

"When the police finally came, I didn't tell them what happened. I couldn't stop crying. My caseworker showed up at the police station saying she had a different foster home for me. On our way there, I begged her to let me go back to my bio dad, but she said he never finished his case reviews.

"She then said, 'I'm sorry, but you're a ward of the state now.'

"When I heard that, I felt a pain in my stomach like a knife. My face must've shown the horror I felt, 'cause she started gushing about how wonderful my new family would be. But I didn't care—I was devastated. I started yelling, 'I don't wanna go. I wanna see my dad. He's the only family I have.'

"My caseworker tried to explain, but words didn't matter. I still had to go."

Heidi's tears poured now.

"At that moment, I knew in my heart there was no one in the world I could trust. Only me. And nobody would ever care about what *I* wanted. That's when I decided to become a runner."

"I feel so bad for you," Shelly said, shaking her head.

"Please don't. It's probably my own fault. My bio dad says I have a way of making everything worse. Anyway, I couldn't risk falling in love with a family again. It hurt too much. On our way there, I started making plans to run away and go back to my dad. I didn't care if he drank and acted like a jerk. I still loved him."

She soaked up tears with her crumpled tissues.

"The good news is my new foster family turned out to be great. They were the best family I ever lived with. The foster mom really loved me, and they all seemed to like having me around."

Heidi started counting on her fingers.

"I lived with seven foster families...and four...no, maybe five group homes. The longest I ever stayed anywhere was two years, and that was with this second family because they actually wanted me. Out of their foster kids, I was the only one they took with them to their new house. I felt so special." Lingering on the memory, she smiled.

Then she groaned.

"I messed it up, though. I met my bio mom and wanted to move in with her. For years, I'd dreamed about meeting her and always hoped to live with her. I thought she might love me if she got to know me.

"But after I moved in, we started fighting—about everything. She got fed up and kicked me out. She didn't care that I had to go back into foster care. She said I disrespected her, which was probably true.

"So much for my dream life," she said with a scoff.

"After that, they put me in a children's home, but that didn't last long either. I broke all their rules. Family Services showed up and placed me with another family. The minute I walked into their house, I could tell they hated me. I remember being jealous of their dogs—they got treated better than me. I kept trying to run away, hoping my caseworker would move me. When she finally did, I never felt so relieved.

"The rest of my foster families are kind of a blur, except for one. My caseworker placed me with a black family, hoping I'd settle down with them. But I didn't. I faked running away and actually hid in their basement for a couple of weeks. They didn't even know it. At night, I'd sneak upstairs and get something to eat.

"One day, while they were all gone, I heard my bio dad's voice on their answering machine. He sounded worried I'd gone missing. Right away, I packed up my bag and got on the highway to hitchhike back to Springfield. I wanted to let him know I was okay.

"I didn't get very far. The police picked me up about a mile down the road and called Family Services. My caseworker came and brought me here to Springfield."

Heidi glanced toward the living room. The noise level in the lodge had increased with people fixing breakfast, getting ready for the day. Hearing a ruckus, I walked over to the doorway and saw several young boys wrestling on the floor.

I turned back toward the ladies. "Excuse me, but I need to go and calm things down."

In the living room I recognized the three brothers, but didn't see their mother anywhere. For safety reasons, we ask parents to stay with their children, especially the younger ones.

"Boys, no wrestling in the house. Where's your mom?"

"I think she's downstairs dressing Theo," the oldest replied.

"Well, you boys need to go down and stay with your mom until she's finished."

I waited.

They scrambled to their feet and scurried toward the basement. On my way back in, I noticed for the first time how exhausted Heidi looked. I hadn't offered her anything to eat or drink. Her story had drawn me in from the moment she said, "I was born homeless."

"Hey, let's take a break," I said. "Heidi, you must be hungry and tired after being out all night."

She nodded, laying the blanket aside.

"Elaine, would you take Heidi to the kitchen and help her find some breakfast?"

"Sure thing." She hopped off the couch and offered a hand to Heidi, pulling her up.

"We can finish your story after you eat and get some rest," I said. "Then we'll go through the intake forms. Shelly has your room key, and I'll get you a locker combination later."

I looked at Elaine. "Can you show Heidi her room after breakfast?"

She gave me a salute. "Yes, sir." She linked her arm with Heidi's and they walked out together. "Let's go find you something to eat."

I looked at the clock. I couldn't believe the day was only getting started.

# SIX

## All Alone in Life

Connie arrived at noon to relieve Shelly. Jacob trotted in behind her with a big smile. "Hi, Dad," he said, flashing his dimples.

"Hey, buddy, how are you?" I gave him a hug. With his four older siblings in school, Jacob loved spending time at the mission.

Connie took his hand and led him toward the back room. "We ate lunch early, so I'm laying Jake down for his nap."

Shelly picked up her bag. "I hate leaving in the middle of Heidi's story, but I can't stay."

"Connie can log the rest this afternoon. Thanks for entering the first part."

"You're welcome. I'm anxious to find out what happens next." Waving goodbye, she left through the front door.

I collected my paperwork and stacked it in my briefcase. Connie returned, taking a seat behind the desk.

"I wish I could stay and tell you about our newest resident," I said, "but I have a meeting next door in the office building. You'll see Heidi's story in the log. It should give you an idea of what we know so far."

She pulled the computer screen closer. "I'll catch up while you're gone."

"I should be back in about an hour. If Heidi comes down, tell her to make herself at home until I get back."

"Sounds good."

My meeting only lasted an hour as I had hoped. Closing the conference room door, I heard people laughing in the main office. I stopped in their doorway.

Four ladies were sitting around a long table with stacks of letters and envelopes piled in front of them. I recognized three of the ladies as volunteers.

"How's everything going?" I asked.

"Great," one replied. "Half the mailing is stuffed, sealed, and ready to go."

"Wow, you ladies are fast. Connie and I just finished the letter yesterday."

"Teena made all the copies this morning," another lady said. "The copier didn't break down once."

Teena's face lit up. "I think this is the best copier we've had yet, Scott."

As our director of operations, Teena wore many hats at the mission. She spent most of her hours in the office building, yet she would sometimes fill in as a lodge supervisor. We'd often find Teena in the lodge during her lunch break rocking one of our babies in the house. Our resident mothers loved that.

"I'm glad it's a good one," I said. "Thank you, ladies, for all your hard work. Looks like our mailing will go out on time as usual."

We had stopped taking government funding years ago, so our ministry depended on these mailings. Each month, we would send out a letter or newsletter to our faithful supporters, updating them on our work with the homeless. Throughout the years, we'd watch God move people's hearts and they would always meet our needs, even in dire circumstances.

"Oh, I almost forgot," I said, walking toward the row of metal file cabinets. "I need to grab a folder." I chatted with the ladies until I found Heidi's paperwork, and headed back to the shelter.

In the lodge I found Connie on the loveseat bagging detergent. She greeted me over a large bucket of dry detergent sitting on the floor between her feet.

"Have you met Heidi?" I asked, opening her file at the desk.

"Not yet." Connie dumped a scoop of detergent into a plastic bag, sealing it. She tossed it into a crate.

"Well, she's probably sleeping. She looked exhausted."

I sifted through Heidi's file and found she'd stayed at the mission almost five years earlier. She had given her baby up for adoption during her two week stay here. I set the file aside and leaned back, stretching. With the lodge quiet, I could take a few minutes to tell Connie about our newest guest.

After filling in the details of Heidi's story, I reflected aloud, "One thing this job has done for me is make me thankful for the families we had growing up."

"I agree," Connie said, tossing another bag in the crate. "I didn't realize how good we had it till we came here."

Right then, we heard noises coming from the back room.

Connie placed the lid on the detergent and stepped over the bucket. "I'd better grab Jacob before he gets into something."

"I'll put these away for you." I reached for the crate and the bucket, hauling them to the back room.

"Hi, Dad," Jacob called out, leaning over his mom's shoulder.

"Hey, buddy." I kissed him on the forehead, and we heard a boisterous laugh coming from the office. It had to be Elaine. Going back in, I found her standing in the doorway with Heidi.

"Come on in, ladies. Have a seat. You look rested, Heidi."

"I feel much better, thank you."

Elaine dropped on the couch beside her. "I feel pretty good myself."

I chuckled.

Connie walked in and settled Jacob on the floor with a bag of toys. Seeing Heidi, he grinned and announced, "I'm Jake."

"Aw, he's cute. I love dimples."

"You just met our fifth child, Jacob, and that's my wife, Connie, carrying our sixth child, due in four months."

"Three months," Connie said, with a gleam in her eyes.

Elaine let out a cackle.

"Taking the clipboard, Connie went to the loveseat. "I'm glad we had room for you, Heidi. You look warm and dry now."

"Yeah, I didn't notice how cold I was until Scott said I could stay. Then I started shaking like a leaf."

I pushed the computer screen out of the way.

"Okay, let's get started. If you don't mind, Heidi, we'd like to hear the rest of your story. We still don't know why you stayed out all night in the rain."

Sitting back, she swept her bangs to one side.

"I'm glad you asked, but I feel kind of strange talking about me. I'm not used to anyone asking about *my* life. Where did I leave off?"

"You said the police picked you up on the highway, and Family Services brought you back here to Springfield."

"Oh, yeah." She gazed out the window, remembering.

"When we got here, my caseworker enrolled me in a youth program and moved me into one of their apartments—which I loved. For the first time in my life, I felt like a grown-up.

"But once again, I did something stupid. I let a guy move in with me. It didn't take long for them to catch him, and they kicked me out of their program.

"I don't know what I was thinking. I had to go right back into foster care. Then, after getting placed with a family, I found out I was pregnant. I felt sorry telling my caseworker 'cause I knew she'd have to move me again. This time, she took me to a maternity home up north for unwed teens.

"That's where I lived before coming to the mission. I could've stayed there longer, but I got into an argument with one of the staff members and punched her. My son, Eli, was two months old at the time."

"You were so young," Connie said. "It must have been hard."

"Yeah, but I knew better. I shouldn't have gotten so angry. The bad thing is it happened right before Christmas and Family Services couldn't find a place for us. Nobody wants a teenager with a baby. That's why we came here. To be honest, I was okay with it. I wanted to be in Springfield and start over and do things right this time.

"I also wanted to surprise my bio mom and show her Eli. I thought she might be happy to have a grandson, and even take us in for awhile."

Tears came to her eyes.

"What'd she say?" Elaine asked, getting tissues for her.

"Not much, really. We arrived at her house and she hardly looked at him. She didn't care at all. We ate supper and talked a little, but as soon as we were done, she brought us back to the mission and drove off without even saying goodbye."

She wiped her sliding tears.

"I felt abandoned all over again. Why am I such a loser?"

Connie looked directly at her. "You're not a loser, Heidi. Your mom is the loser. She lost you, and I feel sad for her."

"Couldn't agree more," Elaine said, with disgust.

I opened her file, flipping through it.

"So what happened while you stayed here? I read something in your file about adoption."

"The day I arrived, I thought Eli had a cold. After a few days, instead of getting better, he got worse. I know this sounds terrible, but I didn't want to take him to a doctor. The last thing I wanted to hear was people saying I was a bad mom. When I got pregnant, people told me I should give my baby up for adoption. They said I was too young to be a good mom. That made me mad, and I wanted to prove them wrong.

"So when Eli got sick, I waited as long as I could. Then someone on staff here said I should take him to a doctor, and that scared me. I ended up taking him to the ER."

Her eyes flooded with tears.

"I'm not proud of this, but when I found out he would be okay, I told the doctor to find a good home for him, and then I walked out. I knew he needed more than what I could give him. I hated myself for doing this, but I didn't want him to have a childhood like mine. Eli deserved better than that. I left the hospital and cried all the way here. I cried for days.

"They had me sign papers later."

Her tears overflowed.

"When I held little Eli for the last time, it was the hardest, sweetest moment of my life. I loved my son with all my heart, but I knew it was selfish to keep him." Her voice trembled. "Now, he has a wonderful family with parents who will cherish him forever."

Heidi lowered her face and wept quietly in her hands.

I glanced around and saw we were all crying. Elaine passed the tissue box. I felt myself wanting to sob just thinking about this young mother's sacrifice.

A minute or two later, Heidi raised her head. She wiped her splotchy face with a wet cloth Connie had given her.

"Are you okay to finish?" I asked. "We can do this later if you want."

"I'll be okay," she said. "I must need to cry or something."

"We don't mind. That's part of your healing."

She folded the cloth, laying it beside her.

"The day I signed the papers, Family Services put me back in foster care. I was sixteen years old and still a ward of the state.

"I remember feeling angry and confused. More than anything, I wanted to see my dad and ask him questions about my life. I needed to know if he or my mom ever really loved me. I'd started having nightmares about my childhood and began waking up terrified every night—"

Her voice cracked.

"Why didn't he love me enough to protect me? And why did my mom abandon me?"

She began weeping again, and Elaine reached over, patting her.

In the background, I heard Jacob playing with his cars, revving the engines without a single care in his small world.

Connie went to the kitchen and came back with a glass of ice water for Heidi. Composing herself, Heidi took a sip. Then she continued.

"When I finally aged out of the system, I celebrated by looking for a job. I couldn't wait to get out on my own. But that turned out to be a joke. Who wants a skinny, half-breed, high school drop-out?"

She looked down at herself. "No one, that's who.

"That is, until I walked into this glitzy-looking place that turned out to be a men's club. They hired me on the spot, no questions asked. The manager assigned me to a dancer called Cinnamon, and she took me under her wing and taught me the business.

"I learned how to dance, how to make men happy, and how to earn money. 'The happier you make the men,' Cinnamon told me, 'the more money you take home.'

"The manager set me up in a small apartment nearby and gave me a fake ID. I called my foster mom—the second one—and told her about my new job. She still cares about me and helps me out whenever she can. I thought she'd be happy to hear my news, but instead, she pleaded with me to quit. I told her I had no choice, and promised I wouldn't do that kind of work forever. My plan was to take advantage of the money while I could, and find a decent job later."

Her eyes followed Jacob's car rolling back and forth on the carpet.

"I just wanted to be in control of my life for once, and this job was my chance.

"The manager of the club ran a tight business. He protected us girls and made sure we had everything we needed to put on a good show. At first, I felt a little embarrassed doing that sort of thing, but I got over it and learned how to make good money."

Heidi's cheeks turned pink.

"My stage name was Vanilla Bean, and since I was new, the other dancers watched over me. They made sure no one gave me any trouble. The club treated me better than my own flesh and blood. I really liked that.

"I also liked the money. I could buy anything I wanted. I had no idea I could make hundreds of dollars a week at my age. Of course, the club got their cut first, then Cinnamon, but I still had plenty left over to buy whatever I needed.

"I loved my new life.

"But then, two years later, they sold the club and replaced our nice manager. That changed everything. The new guy ran the club all-business-like, not caring about us dancers. All he cared about was the almighty dollar.

"I'm glad I had my own place by then. As soon as I'd started bringing in good money, they told me I was on my own. I lived with a guy for awhile, but then I leased my apartment and moved out. After that, I bought a brand new car and opened a savings account. I couldn't believe I still had money left over. I can't say I liked the club as much, but I could take care of myself, and had no problem bringing in cash.

"Then a scary thing happened.

"While giving this guy a private dance, he reached out and grabbed me. No one had ever done that before. It terrified me. I tried backing away, but he wouldn't let go. The dude was scrawny, but mean. He kept saying, 'I paid for my time, and I'm getting what I came for.'

"I pushed him away, and he raised his fist at me. I let out a scream. Another client, hearing our scuffle, rushed over and pulled him back. I jumped out of the way just in time. A fight broke out between them.

"Seconds later, a bouncer ran in and broke up the fight. Next, the manager came and threw both guys out. He pointed his finger at me and said, 'Leave. You no longer work here.' I pleaded with him, but he ordered us all off the property. It happened so fast, I was in shock. He gave me two minutes to grab my stuff and get out.

"I literally ran out of the club to my car and threw my bags in the backseat. I stood beside my car, shaking, trying to catch my breath. Then I heard a car pulling up behind me. I turned around and saw the client who had defended me earlier sitting in a brand new Corvette.

"He rolled down his window and said, 'Hey, I'm really sorry about your job. My name is Ted, and I'd like to make you an offer. I'll pay you a weekly salary if you come to my house and work.'

"I started to back away.

"He held up his hand. 'Wait, it's not like that. My wife is sick. I need someone to care for her while I'm at work. We have a large house with a small apartment in the back where you can stay. It has its own private entrance.'

"I didn't answer. My heart was still pounding.

"Ted held out his business card and said, 'I know you're upset right now. Just take my card and think about it. If you're interested, call me by the end of the week. I need someone soon.'

"I drove home shaken from the whole experience. I'd been in rough spots before, but this time really scared me. I wanted to stop dancing altogether. More than anything, I wanted to find a decent way to make money. Ted's offer sounded like the answer I was looking for.

"So the next day, I called him. I didn't want to lose this opportunity. Ted picked up the phone and got excited when he found out it was me. He asked me to stop by that evening to meet his wife, Barbara.

"The idea of going to his house alone scared me, so I looked up a bartender friend my dad hired years ago and asked her to go with me. Everyone calls her Cappie, and she knows how to handle people. I told her Ted seemed nice, but I didn't feel safe going alone. Cappie was glad to go, saying she could use a little adventure in her life.

"Later, when we got there, Ted gave us a tour of his house and apartment. Everything was just as he'd said. I'd have my own private entrance and get paid three hundred and fifty bucks a week. He showed me Barbara's daily schedule and her list of medicines. He told me I'd be fixing meals for her and doing light housekeeping.

"Everything about the job sounded perfect. Growing up, I had lots of experience cooking and cleaning. At least now I'd get paid for it and help someone in need. Cappie agreed, saying the job seemed tailor-made for me.

"Right away, Barbara and I connected, and before the night

was over, I accepted Ted's offer. Two days later, I moved into the apartment and began working full-time. I couldn't have been happier. Ted and Barbara seemed to really care about each other. They never had children, but their lives were happy and full until she got cancer."

The office phone rang, jarring me back to the present. I answered it and transferred the call to the living room for one of our residents. "Sorry about that. Go ahead."

She let out a deep sigh. "I'm almost done."

"From the start, I loved my new job. While Ted traveled for work, Barbara and I got really close. I could tell she liked having me around, which made me feel like part of their family. I hoped to stay there a long time.

"But last night, everything fell apart." She glanced at Jacob, lowering her voice.

"After supper, Ted and Barbara invited me to their living room to watch TV. I'd done that before and felt comfortable saying yes. Except this time in the middle of a show, Ted turned the volume way down and sat next to me on the couch.

"It seemed a little weird, but with Barbara in the room, I wasn't worried. Ted had always been a friendly guy. He turned to me and said, 'Heidi, we love having you here. Barbara and I can't believe how well you fit into our lives. Everything's going smoother than we hoped.'

"He reached over and patted my knee, which surprised me, but I thought he was just being nice. Then he moved closer and said, 'I want you to know how much we appreciate your friendship. We both feel like we've known you forever.'

"Next, I felt his hand on my back."

"Yikes," Elaine said, raising an eyebrow.

"A chill went up my spine, but I wanted to trust him. He and Barbara had been so good to me. And then he started rubbing my shoulders and said, 'We want you to take on one more special duty of the house.'

Connie stopped writing. "Oh no, what did you say?"

Heidi blushed.

"I said, 'Sure, whatever you want,' hoping it wasn't a big deal. I'd lived there almost seven weeks. They felt like family to me."

Elaine lunged forward. "So what'd he want? What'd he ask?"

"Well, Ted moved in real close and whispered in my ear, 'How about taking on Barbara's wifely duties, starting tonight?'"

Elaine squealed, flinging herself back.

"Yeah, my heart skipped a beat. I looked over and saw Barbara smiling like the cat in *Alice in Wonderland*. I wasn't sure what *that* meant, but I had a pretty good idea.

"So I asked Ted, 'Barbara's wifely duties? What do you mean?'

"He gave me this creepy look and said, 'Heidi, we *both* really like you, and I haven't had a woman in my bed since Barbara's diagnosis. We're asking you to…'"

The ladies' mouths fell open.

"I didn't hear the rest. I shoved him away and jumped off the couch. Then I burst into tears and ran out of the house. Ted called my name, but I ran faster."

Tears streamed down Heidi's face.

"Why did I think things could be different? My new perfect life shattered right before my eyes. I'm so tired of—" She began sobbing. "What's wrong with me? Why can't anything good work out for me?"

Elaine wrapped her arm around Heidi. Jacob stopped making engine noises and watched. We all waited.

"All night long, I've been walking in the rain, wondering what to do. I can't go back there. Why are strings always attached? I thought they wanted to be my family.

"Now I have no job and no place to go."

Heidi, sponging her face with the cloth, looked at me.

"Do you think I can stay here awhile? I am completely alone and on my own."

Her luminous green eyes, gazing into mine, almost made me forget her question. Here was a young woman, distressed and alone, sitting in a homeless shelter. In my world, she'd be looking forward to a college diploma, a good career, or life with a young man.

"Scott?"

"Of course you can stay," I said, focusing. "That's why we're here. Do you plan on going back and getting your belongings? What about your car?"

Her hands began to tremble. "No, I don't care about my stuff. I don't want Ted to know where I'm at. He might talk me into going back. I just need someone to go and pick up my car while Ted is at work."

"Okay, we can take care of that."

Outside the window, I saw people carrying bags of groceries up our front steps. The doorbell rang.

Connie set her clipboard aside and stood. "Thank you for sharing your story with us, Heidi. You've had scary things happen in your life. Try to relax while you're here. This is a safe place."

She took Jacob's hand and led him to the front door. I heard her invite the group in and escort them to the downstairs pantry.

I turned my attention back to Heidi.

"Please understand, you can move out anytime you want. My hope is that you'll stay here long enough to find some answers for your life."

"I need to stay for awhile," she said. "I have to find a new job."

"Are you ready to go through the intake process?"

"I think so."

I opened the packet, and fifteen minutes later, she signed our last form.

Taking that as her cue, Elaine sprang from the couch and turned toward Heidi. "Hey, I'm going outside to smoke. Come with me—the sun is shining. You'll feel better."

Accepting her offer, Heidi stopped at the desk before going out. "Thank you for everything."

"You're welcome. I'm glad we can help you."

Watching them leave, I felt grateful for Elaine's kindness toward Heidi. Despite her own issues, Elaine had wonderful people skills. Perhaps she could help Heidi understand she's not the only person feeling all alone in life.

# SEVEN

## Deeper Than a Bandage

For several days, I mulled over Heidi and Elaine's stories. Neither had fallen into homelessness overnight. Each had a unique journey, yet both were broken. I had to wonder, if these ladies are the face of homelessness, then how could anyone believe jobs, money, and housing are the solution?

"We may not understand the root cause of homelessness," I told Connie one evening at home, "but we know it goes much deeper than the lack of a job, money, or a house."

"I agree," she said. "Elaine and Heidi both had jobs, but that didn't keep either one from becoming homeless."

"Yeah, and they both had money. Elaine confessed this morning she had inherited $350,000 from her parents' estate almost seven years ago."

Connie's eyes widened. "Are you kidding?"

"It's all gone now. She spent it on drugs, alcohol, and food for huge blow-out parties lasting days at a time. She also bought a brand new car, nice clothes, and entertainment for her daughters and a few of their friends to keep them busy while she partied."

She gasped.

"Elaine said the money lasted less than four years. She cried pretty hard telling us about it this morning. When the money ran out, she said her party friends all disappeared, and her seventeen year old daughter, Carrie, moved out for good."

"Poor Elaine. She learns lessons the hard way."

"It just shows how money, in any amount, doesn't help a person make good decisions in life. After four years of nonstop partying, Elaine had to go back to work. But she couldn't keep a job because of her addictions. She eventually lost her house *and* custody of her younger daughter."

"Wow, that's terrible."

"You know, I've been thinking about this all day. If Elaine hadn't inherited the money, she would've hit rock bottom much sooner—and that would've forced her to face her issues years ago. Her addictions could be history now. But instead of getting the help she needed, she received money."

"Which only prolonged her destructive behavior," Connie said.

"Exactly."

I had to get out of my chair. I process better on my feet, and Connie doesn't mind my pacing.

"Material assets in themselves couldn't keep her afloat," I said, "which means the real cause of Elaine's homelessness isn't physical. It's something deeper. We thought Elaine's job would make all the difference, but if anything, it made things worse."

"We thought we were helping. We had good intentions."

"Yeah, and so do many others in this field of work. Yet jobs and money aren't solving the issues."

I circled the dining room.

"So what should we do?" she asked. "We aren't helping people long term."

"Well, we don't need to expand the mission yet. How can we add more rooms if we don't have solutions? We're supposed to vote on expansion next week at the board meeting. How can I tell our trustees I no longer agree with my own expansion ideas? That should be a special moment."

I sank into my chair.

"Well, Scott, we've been praying for understanding for weeks. We may not have all the answers, but we know homelessness isn't solved by what we're doing. The physical stuff isn't working. The trustees need to hear that, and hopefully, understand." She picked up a ball on the floor and bounced it my direction.

"You're right," I said, catching it, "but I might be looking for a new job if the conversation doesn't go well. Don't forget, our last two executive directors had to leave after heated boardroom discussions. Are you ready for our family to move if something goes wrong?"

I dribbled the ball, ruminating on the possibility.

My mind went to Rachel, our oldest child. I'll never forget the day she asked me if she would always be the new kid in school. My heart almost broke. Before we had moved to this area, Rachel had attended three different schools in four years. Now she was happily settled in our small school district north of Springfield. The idea of digging ditches sounded better than moving her again.

"Of course I don't want to move," Connie replied, "but you have to tell the trustees what we're seeing. People are falling back into homelessness. If you ask them for more time, I believe God will give us the answers we need."

"I need to present a compelling reason for slowing down this project."

"I think you already have one, but I'll pray for you. Just don't worry about us. God will take care of our family. He always has in the past."

I tossed the ball into a basket of toys.

Hearing Connie's words, I could finally relax. I needed her

support in this, especially with the risk involved. Now I could focus on the upcoming board meeting.

*Lord, give me the right words to speak next week. Help the trustees understand. In Jesus' name.*

Walter, our chairman of the board, called the meeting to order. Fourteen years earlier, he had helped establish the mission. He would serve on our board for two decades. Now an older gentleman and finding it hard to hear, Walter had a reputation for being compassionate, yet stern. He liked answers, and he wanted them straight to the point.

I knew my words would have to count.

Opening with prayer, Walter led us through the agenda, item by item. All nine trustees sat around our conference room table, each representing a supporting church. With only one item left to cover—the vote on expansion—Walter leaned back, folding his hands.

Earlier, I had asked him for permission to address the board prior to the vote. Now, with everything else completed, my time had come.

Walter nodded, giving me the floor.

My mouth felt dry.

Not wanting to waste anyone's time, I jumped in. "I've been praying and thinking a lot these past two weeks, and I believe we need to slow down our plans for expansion."

I took a drink of water, letting my words settle.

"We provide everything a person might need to get out of homelessness: food, shelter, clothing, transportation, and more. But it's not enough. We aren't seeing lasting change.

"Like all of you, Connie and I believed the reason for homelessness was a lack of something physical, such as a job, money, or a house. We assumed if we could help people acquire these things, they would stabilize and overcome homelessness. That hasn't been the case."

"What do you mean?" Walter asked, scowling.

"They use up or lose whatever we help them obtain. With their addictions and poor decision-making, most are falling back into homelessness."

"I don't understand why you're talking about this," Roy, our oldest trustee, said. "Why aren't you focusing on numbers? People want to know *how many* people we shelter each night, *how many* meals we serve, and *how many* children we help."

Roy waved an arthritic hand. "We need to tell people *what* we're providing and *how much*, especially when it comes to the children. People love to help kids. That's how we can expand the mission and help more folk. Isn't that what we've been talking about all along, helping more folk?"

Roy fixed his eyes on me.

"Yes," I said, carefully, "but what if helping people acquire material assets brings more harm than good? What if money and material possessions act like a bandage over a cancerous lesion? The person may look and feel better for a time, but the bandage covers the real problem underneath that's much deeper, that's festering and growing."

I glanced around the table. "Do we want to spend our time and resources replacing bandage after bandage, while ignoring the real surgery needed for recovery?"

Roy grunted and sat back.

"Let me tell you about two of our residents," I said, taking a moment to describe Elaine and Heidi's unique paths to the mission. I gave the trustees an overview of each.

"As you can see, both ladies have festering wounds from their past, and both have underlying issues that led them into homelessness. They aren't the only ones. Nearly all of our residents are trapped in a cycle of gaining, and then losing, their money, material goods, and housing. Their lives are unstable and miserable. Any event or crisis, even minor, sends them back into homelessness.

"In light of this, I think we have two choices. We can continue giving out physical stuff—and sleep good at night knowing we gave to the homeless—or we can try to figure out what's going on underneath and help them out of this cycle forever."

Several eyebrows went up.

"Our country provides all kinds of bandages to the needy: programs, housing assistance, food stamps, and more. Yet poverty and homelessness are getting worse, not better. Especially for women and children.[1] I believe the real issues get buried underneath a pile of stuff that makes their lives look better for awhile, but doesn't last.

"The truth is, money and material goods give people false hope and make them believe their lives *are* better. Except their behavior isn't changing. They end up losing everything *again*, and they feel like even bigger failures.

"I'll give you an example.

"About two weeks ago Elaine started a new job at a restaurant here in town. On her first night waiting tables, she earned a good amount of tip money in cash. When the night was over, instead of returning to the mission, she stayed out all night using crack.

"The next day Elaine came back stoned and penniless, which shocked me. It made me re-evaluate my motives and everything we do at the mission. I began praying for insight and read Matthew 6:33, which says, 'But seek first his kingdom and his righteousness, and all these things will be added to you.'[2]

"That verse hit me right between the eyes. I felt God calling us to spend time seeking *him* before we expand or do anything else."

I looked at each person around the table. Every trustee on our board had a heart for the homeless, and they all hoped to help our hurting residents in some way.

"We cannot just *hope* people will get better," I said. "If we truly care about them, we will seek God's kingdom first and pray for wisdom to understand homelessness.

"I believe that's the key to unlocking this broken world. And once we understand the root cause, we can find lasting solutions. *Then* we can raise money for expansion."

Walter, taking a deep breath, exhaled slowly. "What you're saying makes sense, Scott, but I wish we'd known all this earlier."

His eyes bore through me.

"Yes, and I owe you all an apology," I said. "I think it took me seeing Elaine's setback firsthand to admit what I didn't want to believe: Our answers don't work.

"I am truly sorry. And now I'm asking you to join me in doing what I should've done in the first place—seek God's kingdom and pray for his wisdom.

"If we don't take time to pray and get answers now," I added, "I'm afraid the mission will become a revolving door of material goods and false hope."

Our board secretary laid his pen down. "Scott, that's the last thing we want to see happen. We want people to find a way out of homelessness just as you do. My question is, how are you going to fix these people once you understand their deeper issues? It sounds complicated to me."

"You're right," I said. "Understanding and fixing are two different things. We cannot begin to think about fixing until we understand their issues first."

Someone said "yes" in the background.

"So with the board's permission, I would like to make the mission a laboratory, of sorts, where we can examine homelessness at its core. In doing this, I believe we will find the answers we're looking for with God's help. After that, we can develop strategies for homeless recovery. I would like for us to become spiritual surgeons, skilled at removing the deeper lesions, instead of experts in covering them up."

A trustee, one of our local ministers, spoke up. "Are you saying the physical stuff is no longer important?"

"Not at all. People often come to us with little more the clothes they're wearing. We still need to provide the basic necessities of life. I'm just saying, when we offer material goods, we should distribute them wisely, and view them as temporary bandages—protective coverings—until the deeper wounds are dealt with."

I noticed the clock, seeing my time had gone.

"Let me end by saying this. Caring people love to help the needy. Many will provide bandages again and again. Churches and agencies do this, following the lead of our government. Please understand, we will be going against the grain of cultural belief to claim that physical provisions—including a house—do not solve their issues long term. We will get criticized.

"Because of this, I want to make sure our analysis of homelessness is accurate and clear. We need to understand the deeper issues and be able to answer any questions that might arise. At the same time, we have to be ready to present solutions that will make a difference."

Winding down, I sat back in my chair.

"I don't know how long this will take or what we'll find exactly, but I'm convinced we need to go this route."

Finished, I looked at Walter. No matter what the trustees might decide, I felt at peace knowing I hadn't forgotten anything. I hoped no one felt overwhelmed. My passion often brings with it a flurry of words.

Walter took the floor.

"Well, Scott, I'd like to see you get out there and raise money as Roy mentioned earlier, but I'm willing to wait and see how you progress. What do the rest of you think?"

He scanned faces around the table.

Our treasurer spoke up. "I have no idea what causes homelessness, but if Scott still has questions after working on the front lines every day, I think we ought to give him a chance to find answers."

Others agreed.

"All right," Walter said, "do we have a consensus to hold off on expansion and let Scott move forward on his exploration of homelessness?"

The trustees approved, unanimous. A wave of relief washed over me.

*Thank you, God, for their support.*

Walter closed his notebook. "Keep us informed of your progress, Scott. Plans for expansion are tabled until further notice."

Walter adjourned the meeting with prayer.

Cleaning up afterward, I could feel my excitement building. I had received the board's approval and couldn't wait to go home and share the news with Connie.

Our quest for understanding homelessness could now officially begin.

# EIGHT

## Something Real

The next morning, I walked through the front door of the lodge feeling more anxious than excited. Connie and I were both overjoyed about the board's decision, but now we had to find answers. We didn't want to let our trustees down.

*Lord, we need your wisdom and knowledge.*

Inside, I found Elaine waiting for me on the living room couch. She plunked down her mug of coffee, throwing aside her newspaper.

"You're up bright and early this morning," I said, veering into the office.

She leaped up, following me. "Do you have time to talk?"

"Yes, but can it wait a half an hour? I'd like to read the log and catch up on the residents." Looking down, I noticed her Pink Panther slippers. On Elaine, they seemed right.

"Okay, I'll come back in thirty minutes." She backed out, pulling the bottom half of the double door shut. It pleased me to see her willing to wait. Patience wasn't a natural gift of hers.

Surprising all of us, Elaine had embraced her six weeks of house restriction with great enthusiasm. She chose to stay on our property, taking on more chores, extra cooking duties, and new reading assignments. To her credit, Elaine had sunk low enough, had hurt enough people in her life that she never wanted to go back. She desired a new way of living.

I chatted with Shelly, our lodge supervisor, now leaving. "Thanks for covering for me," she said. "I'll be back after my daughter's eye appointment."

"See you then."

At the mission, we follow a laid-back policy when it comes to family. We try to accommodate each other's needs whenever possible.

I pulled the computer screen closer, reading the log. Next, I sorted through mail.

In my periphery, I saw Elaine heading for the office couch with her newspaper. I'm sure she didn't think I would notice her early arrival, but her bigger-than-life personality rattled every doorknob and piece of furniture.

I finished reading a letter addressed to me, and set the mail aside. I had no idea God was about to reveal the first teacher we needed to understand homelessness, and she wore Pink Panther slippers.

"So what's on your mind today?" I asked, leaning back, clasping my hands behind my head.

Elaine had spent many hours with us during the past three weeks opening up about her life. She talked about her shame and guilt, saying it clung to her like a cold, damp fog, trying to suffocate her.

"Well, as you know," she said, in her most serious tone, "I've been evaluating my life. This morning I woke up with a horrible realization. I don't know how to have normal relationships with people. Especially men. Now don't get me wrong, I've had my chances through the years—more men than you care to know about—but none of them filled the emptiness in my heart or made me happy."

That didn't surprise me. I just nodded.

"From the time I was a child, the one thing I wanted more than anything else was my father's attention. He worked long hours and flew out of town on business each week. I rarely saw him. He'd come home after my bedtime and leave early the next morning. Mom talked about him like he was part of our family, but in my world, he didn't exist.

"The only time I saw Dad was after a long business trip. He'd walk into the house, drop money and presents on the table for us kids, and disappear into his study. What I really wanted was a chance to sit on his lap and talk. Be a part of his life. I don't remember ever having a conversation, just the two of us. All my friends did stuff with *their* fathers, even if their parents were divorced. But my dad never had time for me."

She pulled out a tissue, wiping her eyes.

"I think I've spent my whole life searching for a man to love me. Nothing ever lasts. I end up hurting every guy before he has a chance to hurt me. I hate doing this, but I'm so afraid of being rejected. What should I do? Do you think I'm broken or something?"

Without hesitation, I offered a phrase I'd heard and used many times in my Christian life. "You need to lay your pain at the feet of the cross and let the love of Jesus wash it away."

She glared. "Now how am I supposed to do that? And what's this love of Jesus you're talking about? I've been loved in every position known to man. How is yours any different?"

She sat back, crossing her arms.

*Whoa, where did that come from?*

I sensed the perfect time to bring up the gospel. With passion and personality, I talked about Jesus, who he was and what he did. "He died on the cross and rose from the dead because he loves you and wants you to go to heaven."

"That's nice," she said, unmoved. "We've talked about that before and it doesn't help me understand love. How do I know if a guy is telling me the truth when he says, 'I love you?' I also need to know what it means when *I* say it."

Her question seemed simple, yet I found no words.

She tried again.

"I know that Jesus died on the cross, but how do I know when love is real? Ask someone to die for me? What good is that? I can't love a corpse."

I stared at her for a moment, stumped.

Then I offered up a quick prayer and dove in. I recited every definition of love I could think of, hoping God would bless my effort.

He didn't.

Elaine squinted at me.

"I don't need a sermon, Scott. I need something real. Something I can use."

I shuffled around in my chair.

"Well, I feel kind of foolish not answering your question. It's obvious I need more time. Let me work on it. I want to give you a definition of love you can use every day."

After a few seconds, she hopped to her feet.

"Okay, let me know if you get it figured out. I really do want to understand, because if it's real, I plan to use it in my life. Maybe then I can accept some of those other Christian ideas you talk about."

She snatched her newspaper and walked out, leaving me alone to face the truth of my platitudes, which had no effect on someone living outside of my belief system.

Elaine deserved better than this.

For the rest of the day I couldn't shake the significance of her question or the memory of my own loftiness when I said, "lay your pain at the feet of the cross and let the love of Jesus wash it all away." I had used that line before and *others* appreciated it. Not Elaine. She wanted something tangible. And real. Something practical for everyday life.

*Lord, how do I get past the jargon of my own beliefs? Have I spent so much time surrounded by fellow believers, I never had to think past our shared understanding of truth?*

Before our conversation that day, I believed I had a pretty good grasp on love. The Bible mentions it hundreds of times, and many of those "love verses" I'd known since childhood. I had recognized the importance of love—how it plays a central role in Christianity—long before I ever stepped foot on a Bible college campus as a freshman.

Yet my answers weighed light on the scales of Elaine's questioning.

I opened my Bible to Matthew 22 and read Jesus' words, "Love the Lord your God with all your heart and with all your soul and with your entire mind…and the second is like it: Love your neighbor as yourself."[1]

For as long as I could remember, I tried to live by this scripture. Why couldn't I explain it to Elaine in a way that made sense?

*God, help me understand your love. Help me go deeper for Elaine.*

For the next two days I searched my Bible, writing down every verse that shed light on the subject. Afterward, I met with Elaine in the lodge office.

I presented my exhaustive study on love, scripture by scripture, saving 1 Corinthians 13 for the climax: "Love is patient, love is kind. It does not envy, it does not boast, it is not proud…"[2] and so on.

Satisfied, I closed my Bible and smiled at Elaine. Surely this answered her question. She had listened without interrupting me once.

Lines etched across her forehead.

"Wow, you spent a lot of time putting this together. I hate to say it, but you didn't answer my question."

I dropped my head back, sighing.

She hurried to add, "I really liked that scripture you ended with, but I'll never remember all those things you listed out. Like I said earlier, I need something simple that can help me understand love. I need to know when it's real. You always say Christianity is practical and relevant. If that's true, then give me something I can use in my everyday life."

*Does she really want to know, Lord, or is this her way of controlling? Maybe she doesn't want an answer.*

I studied her face for a clue. Nothing. Then I heard a faint nudging.

*This isn't just for Elaine.*

Well, then, who? I wondered.

Seconds later, I knew. I had to find the answer for *me*. How could I claim to be a Christian if I didn't understand the essence of my own beliefs? Elaine's motives didn't matter. I had to define the most significant aspect of my belief system in a practical, relevant way that made sense to *me* first. Only then could I possibly help someone else understand.

I rolled my chair back, and stood.

"I believe there's a better answer out there, but I need more time."

We held eye contact for a few seconds.

"Well, I hope you bring me something I can use," she said, standing. "I really mean that. My future depends on it."

With that, she turned and marched out of the office.

# NINE

## Practical, Relevant Love

Hearing her last words, I no longer believed Elaine purposely challenged me. Like that Johnny Lee song, she'd spent years "looking for love in all the wrong places."[1] Now she wanted something real. I couldn't wait to get home and search my Bible. A simpler answer had to be there.

Driving home that evening, I wondered about her request. Did a clear-cut explanation of God's love even exist? The apostle John says love not only comes from God, but God *is* love.

*Lord, how can that be? Help me understand your essence. I need to know what it means for us here on earth.*

A question interrupted my prayer.

*What about John 3:16?*

"Everyone knows that verse," I said aloud. "I memorized it as a child."

*Look at it closer. Spend time with it and see what you find.*

At the house, I explained to Connie and the kids I wouldn't be eating supper with them. "I'm sort of on a mission," I said. "It might take awhile, so please pray for me. I hope to accomplish it tonight."

I went to my desk, opening my Bible to John 3:16, and read, "For God so loved the world, he gave his only Son, that whoever believes in him, will not perish but have eternal life."[2]

Those familiar words of my youth are some of the best-known in the Bible. Simplistic, yet profound in what they represent. I read them again.

*What am I missing, Lord?*

I sat at my old wooden desk, pondering and praying over this verse with only one aim: to understand God's love in a practical, relevant way. I didn't bother to turn on my usual background music and soon lost all awareness of time.

That night I stopped only to eat the bowl of vegetable soup Connie set on my desk. I felt sure an answer lay hidden in that passage of scripture, and I was determined to find it.

By the time the sun shone brightly in my room that morning, I finally grasped what I believed God wanted me to see. But would Elaine accept it? Could she find significance in my explanation, or was I still hindered by platitudes and church-speak?

With renewed energy, I walked into the kitchen and ate a quick breakfast with the kids. I promised Connie we would talk later.

I drove to the mission feeling excited, yet nervous. Pulling into the alley behind the lodge, I parked my van next to the white garage and unloaded several bags of clothing my neighbor had dropped off at my home. Next, I took out my briefcase and locked the van.

Walking toward the lodge, I heard a school bus honking out front. The back door of the lodge flew open and kids sprinted down the steps. Several mothers followed, making sure their children boarded the bus safely.

I greeted two women sitting on our back deck smoking. "Beautiful day, isn't it?"

They nodded through their puffs of smoke. I climbed the red

staircase leading up to the kitchen. Don, a lodge supervisor in his fifties, met me at the back door.

"Good morning, Boss," he said, in his familiar, cheery way. He stepped back, letting me enter. "You're here early today."

"Yeah, I couldn't sleep and decided to come on in. How are things here?"

"Oh, the usual." Don checked his watch. "I'm driving Beverly to the dentist this morning. Someone just called from their office asking us to arrive early. Do you mind if we go ahead and leave?"

I rested my overstuffed briefcase on a kitchen chair. "That's fine with me. I wanted to get started early anyway."

"Let me log one more thing," he said, "then I'll go find Bev. I think she's out back enjoying her last smoke before the big extraction." Don grinned, showing a mouthful of white teeth. "Glad it's not me."

I poured a cup of coffee and talked with one of our dads in the shelter who was feeding his toddler some oatmeal.

When Don finished up and departed with Bev, I took over the desk. As usual, I caught up on the log first. After that, I answered phone messages and sorted through mail. I wanted to free up my morning as soon as possible to meet with Elaine.

Clearing the desk, I laid my Bible open at John 3:16, and left the office to go find her. She almost ran me over in the living room.

"Whoa, Elaine, what's the hurry? Do you have time to talk this morning?"

"I just started a load of laundry and realized I'm out of detergent. I have three loads to wash. Can I go in and grab some real quick?"

"Go ahead." She rushed past me into the office to the back supply closet. She came out with three small bags of detergent.

"Let me dump one in the washer and I'll be right back. I'm free after that."

While Elaine dashed downstairs, I read over John 3:16 again. A minute later, she plopped on the office couch, winded. This time I noticed her Lion King tee shirt, Ninja Turtles sweat pants, and neon orange headband. Glancing down, I saw her Pink Panther slippers. I had to smile.

"Hey, it's laundry day," she said, with a laugh.

I chuckled, moving on.

"Well, I think I might have an answer to your question about love."

Her eyebrows shot up. "Really?"

"Remember when I mentioned John 3:16 the other day? 'For God so loved the world, he gave his only Son, that whoever believes in him, will not perish but have eternal life?'"

"Of course. And I don't like it."

"Why not?"

"I hear it quoted at AA meetings. I think it's the only Bible verse people in recovery know. Guys use it for pick-up lines. You know, 'Love is giving—the Bible says so—which means you have to give me what I want.'"

Elaine scrunched her nose.

"You get the picture. Anyway, I've been hurt by that word more than any other in the dictionary, so I hope you have something more. If you don't, I'll be grateful you let me stay here and all, but I'm done talking about your Christian love. I need to make *real* changes in my life."

I held my hand up. "Slow down a minute. We can always find people willing to manipulate scripture for selfish reasons, but that's not what this verse means.

"Before I explain, I want to thank you for pushing me past my comfort level. You made me examine my beliefs and fall on my knees before God. Even though your question surprised me, I appreciate your forthrightness."

Her hearty laugh echoed through the lodge. "You know I'm more demanding than forthright."

Now, *my* laugh echoed.

"Okay, let me show you what I found in John 3:16. I'd like for us to look at this verse one phrase at a time. When we put it back together, I believe you'll find a practical, simple definition of love you can use every day."

Elaine grabbed a couch pillow, stuffing it behind her back.

"Are we ready?"

"I am now," she said, scooching into it.

"The first two words are, 'For God.' What comes to mind when you hear the word, 'God?'"

"I think of perfection. Someone perfect who knows everything."

"Great, I can't think of a better way to describe God. This sets the stage for what comes next. What follows godly or supernatural perfection in this sentence?"

I handed her my Bible, pointing to the verse. She peered closer.

"Look at the next two words, 'so loved.' These words provide the *action* of perfection. When Perfection acts, he always acts in love. But we'll talk about love in a minute. Let's go on to the next two words, 'the world.' Here, we find the *object* of Perfection's love. What comes to mind when you hear the words, 'so loved the world?'"

"I think it means loving everything in the world," Elaine said, "especially people."

"I agree. Now when we put the words together, 'For God so loved the world,' he's saying, 'Okay, listen up. I, God, Perfection, am about to show you my perfect love for humanity. Pay attention and try to understand.'"

She searched the text.

"Look at the next part, 'He gave.' What does it mean?"

"That's the part I don't like," she blurted.

"I know, but notice there's no period after the word, 'gave.' What did God give?"

"His only son."

"*That*, I believe, is the key to perfect love."

She sighed. "I already know about Jesus dying on the cross. Why do we keep talking about that? It doesn't help me understand love in my own life." She tossed her hands up.

"Stay with me, Elaine. *What* was Jesus?"

She raised an eyebrow like I was losing it. "He was God's son."

"You're right. Jesus was God's son, but I didn't ask *who* was Jesus. I asked *what* was Jesus."

Her face went blank.

"Let me explain. Jesus was, and still is, *what was needed*. For God so loved the world, he gave us what *we* needed. Do you understand what that means? Perfect Love isn't just 'giving' to mankind. It's deeper than that. At the right moment in history, God gave us a perfect sacrifice that could take away our sin and bring salvation to the world.

"Think about that, because it's the first part of your definition: 'Love is giving what is needed.' Can you imagine how many marital issues would be resolved if spouses gave exactly what the other person needed?"

"But how can we know what the other person needs?" she asked, swatting a curl out of her eyes.

"That's a great question. Let's look at the second part of John 3:16: 'whoever believes in him will not perish but have eternal life.' That shows the desired outcome of God's love. He wants to give us eternal life. What do you think about when you hear those words?"

"Heaven, of course. But I don't spend much time thinking about it."

"Why not?"

"Everyone has a different idea, but who really knows? I guess I'm more concerned about the other place, since that's where people say I'm going."

"You're right."

"You think I'm going there, too?" she asked, wide-eyed.

I chuckled.

"That's not what I'm saying. You're right about people having their own ideas about heaven. Scripture gives us clues, but let's go back to the sentence, 'whoever believes in him will not perish but have eternal life.' What is eternal life?"

"I suppose living forever in a place called heaven." She shrugged. "Whatever that means."

"Well, the book of Revelation says there'll be no mourning, no crying, and no death in heaven.[3] The pain and heartaches of this life will be gone forever. That means heaven is a place of eternal joy and peace. God wants to give us joy and peace that never ends. *That's* what Perfect Love does.

"Now if we put it all together, we have a definition that describes the kind of love we should have for each other. It's the same kind of love God has for us, only *his* love is perfect. So here's your definition: 'Love is giving what is needed for lasting joy and peace.'"

I gave her a few seconds.

"The way we do this," I said, "is by seeking God and asking for his help. We're told in the book of James to pray for wisdom, and God who is faithful will give it to us.[4]

"That's called living by the Spirit.[5] As we go through life, we ask God for wisdom and wait for his Holy Spirit to reveal it to us."

"Jesus explains more about the Holy Spirit in the book of John. He says God's Spirit will teach us all things.[6] He was talking to his disciples, but he extends that teaching to all believers everywhere.[7] That means we, too, can receive God's wisdom through his Spirit and learn to love people the way Jesus did."

Elaine shoved the loose curl under her headband.

"The problem is, we humans aren't very good at love. We go through life taking what we want, or we give something *we ourselves* want. We transfer our own desires onto the people around us. Most of us have no idea what someone else really needs for lasting joy and peace."

I slid forward, resting my arms on the desk.

"When a guy says he loves you, Elaine, ask yourself, 'Does he care about my long-term wellbeing—my lasting joy and peace— or is he simply offering a momentary high with promises of fun?' Too often, the 'fun' fades away, and all you have left are painful memories."

"I know that one," she murmured.

"What would happen if husbands and wives spent more time trying to understand and provide each other's needs instead of their own? What if a father spent more time caring about his child's wellbeing instead of making a name for himself in the business world?"

Elaine's eyes welled with tears.

"I would like that kind of love, that kind of father."

I handed her tissues. "That's the kind of love our Father in heaven offers to each one of us. It's the same kind of love he wants us to show each other. It's an unselfish love that seeks to bring joy and peace into other people's lives.

"The good news is God offers that love to you right now if you're willing to accept it."

Considering the idea, her eyes went to the seascape hanging on our office wall. I wondered if she could visualize God's love in the white-capped, foamy waves.

In the stillness, I could hear children out front playing.

"I'll be right back." I left the office and stepped out on the front porch. "Girls, you need to take your bicycles around back where your parents can see you."

"Yes, Mr. Payne," they chanted together.

I watched them peddle to the back yard and hollered out a "thank you" before closing the door. In the office, I found Elaine on her feet rearranging couch cushions.

"Well, what do you think?" I asked. "Can you use the definition, 'Love is giving what's needed for lasting joy and peace,' in your own life?"

Plopping down, she yanked off her orange headband. She raked a few curls with her fingers.

"I think so, but this is a whole new way of thinking for me. I'm still trying to figure out what joy and peace means."

Stretching out her headband, she put it back on.

"Okay, it does help me understand love better."

"That's what I hoped."

"I'll have to see how it plays out in my life," she added. "I'll pray for wisdom like you said, but don't be surprised if I have more questions."

"I would be disappointed if you didn't."

Inside, I was jumping up and down, praising God. I knew he'd given us this revelation.

We spent the rest of the morning talking about God's love and the salvation he offers through Jesus. Later that afternoon, Elaine accepted Jesus Christ as her Lord and Savior, and I had the wonderful privilege of baptizing her at our local church.

"It's a brand new beginning for me," she said, whooping with joy. "I feel lighter than I ever have in my whole life."

The conversations I had with Elaine that week would forever change our work at the mission. She was the catalyst I needed to dig deeper into scripture and search out God's practical, relevant truth. Although, we didn't fully understand the root cause of homelessness, the revelation of God's practical love became an important piece in the puzzle of homeless recovery.

And Elaine soon had an opportunity to put it into practice.

# TEN

## The Love Test

Less than a week after Elaine's new beginning, she rushed into the office sobbing. Trying to speak, she could only sputter.

I pushed my keyboard aside. "Slow down, Elaine. What's the matter?"

"My daughter, Carrie, just called from the hospital. She's in the emergency room with Benjamin. He's sick, and he can't breathe."

She let out a wail.

"I have to leave right now and go to the hospital to be with my grandson. He needs me."

"What do you mean, he needs you? Are you a nurse?" I found it best to stay grounded in this job, especially during emotional moments.

"Are you kidding? This is serious."

She charged toward me at the desk.

"I'm dead serious," I said, hoping she planned to stop. "Did Carrie ask you to come to the hospital?"

Elaine halted. "Well, no. She has other people with her."

"Then why do you have to be there?"

"Because he's my grandson. He *needs* me." She wailed again, blowing into a soggy tissue.

"You should stay here. You aren't off house restriction yet. The best thing you can do for Benjamin is wait here and pray for him."

Elaine heaved a sigh, placing her hands on her hips. "How can you keep me from my grandson? He's sick, and he's in the hospital."

Tears covered her exasperated face.

"It's your right to leave whenever you want. I can't stop you. Just understand if you go, I will give your room to someone else. You won't be able to return for at least a month."

I held out a box of tissues.

She grabbed it, huffing. "How can you do this to me?"

"It's simple. I love you, and I want to give you what you need for lasting joy and peace. Carrie called to inform you. She didn't call for you to run to the hospital. I understand you're worried, and rightly so, but the last thing your daughter needs is for you to show up and create an emotional scene, because you're the *grandma*."

Elaine calmed, trying to process.

"Wherever you go, you draw attention to yourself. Every room you enter becomes your stage. *Your* desires, *your* feelings, move into the limelight no matter what else is going on."

Elaine stared at me, at my audacity. But this situation proved to be a perfect teaching moment. I wanted her to learn how to stop herself, how to step back in a situation. Self-restraint isn't easy for anyone, but Elaine needed to understand how unbridled emotion fuels poor decision-making and affects every person around her.

"Instead of going to the hospital, I suggest you stay here and find a quiet place to pray. They need to focus on Benjamin, not you. If you want to give your grandson what he needs most, pray for him. Then wait for an answer."

Her scowl began to soften. This approach was new for Elaine, far removed from her usual grandstanding.

Okay, I'll stay," she mumbled, mopping her eyes, "but I'm not happy about it. I don't know how long I can wait. Can I at least call Carrie and tell her I'm not coming to the hospital?"

I hit a button on the phone. "Line one is ready."

She traipsed into the living room, making the call. Afterward, there was silence. I walked in and found her slouched by the phone.

"So?"

"Carrie agrees with you. She said the emergency room is small and I'd have to wait in the lobby. She's glad I'm staying here. She promises to call as soon as they know something."

"What will you do in the meantime?"

"I'm going upstairs to pray and read. This is new for me, Scott, but maybe I need to try something different."

She brushed past me and clomped up to her room.

The lodge grew quiet.

I went back to the desk, resuming my work. An hour later, the office phone rang. Transferring the call to the living room, I soon heard Elaine racing down the stairs, shouting, "I'll get it!"

Seconds later, she cried out, "He's okay! My grandson's all right! God answered my prayer!"

Walking into the living room, I nearly tripped over Elaine. She sat cross-legged on the floor with tears streaming down her face.

"I prayed hard, for what seemed like forever," she said. "Every minute killed me. I didn't know if Benjamin would live or die. I found a scripture in Psalms about God being our refuge and protector. I begged him to protect Benji, and he *did*."

Several residents gathered around.

"Carrie said he had an allergic reaction to kiwi. I didn't know anyone could be allergic to kiwi, but his bronchial tubes almost shut. They got him to the hospital just in time. He's breathing fine and sleeping now. Carrie said they're keeping him overnight.

"She wants to bring him by here tomorrow when he gets discharged. Is that okay?"

"Sounds great," I said. "I think you're ready to see them. They'll be your first visitors here."

I reached down, patting her shoulder. "You made the right decision today. I know it wasn't easy, and I'm proud of you."

"You were right, Scott. I didn't have to be in the middle of everything. Staying here and praying worked out better."

Suddenly, her face lit up.

"Wow, it actually worked. I gave my daughter what *she* needed most by giving her space, and I gave Benjamin what *he* needed most by praying. I'm so excited. God answered my prayer!"

Elaine leaped up, hugging me. "I'm really glad you didn't let me go to the hospital like I wanted. The same thing always happens at times like these. Sooner or later, I say something to upset my daughter. She gets angry, and we both say terrible things to each other. Afterward, I feel guilty and go out and use. Then I hate myself for days."

Taking a step back, she looked into my eyes.

"Thank you for slowing me down. Instead of causing problems, I actually did something good for once. I think I'm starting to understand how this love thing works."

"Congratulations, you passed your first real test. I couldn't be happier for you."

She flung her arms around me, squeezing like a vice. Then, twirling around, she strutted toward the back door. "I'm going outside to smoke. Now that Benjamin's okay, I can relax and feed the squirrels with Miss Daisy."

Chuckling, I returned to the office picturing Miss Daisy and Elaine tossing out tidbits to squirrels. Miss Daisy would often take her breaks from sorting clothes on the back porch of the old cottage. Without fail, a resident or two would join her. Together, they'd talk about life, and Miss Daisy would offer them sage advice. She'd also extend her big heart to every animal on the property. In her mind, strays didn't exist.

The following morning Elaine rushed into the office, frantic. "Carrie and Benjamin are coming in half an hour!"

Connie laid her newspaper aside. "That's wonderful."

"No, it's not," Elaine said, with bulging eyes. "Well, yes, it is, but I haven't seen them since Carrie dropped me off almost five weeks ago. I don't know what to do."

"Be yourself," I suggested, standing by the copier. I closed the paper tray drawer and hit start.

Her hands flew up. "That always gets me into trouble."

Connie slid over, inviting Elaine to join her on the couch. "You're so much wiser now. You keep learning and taking everything to heart. I haven't seen anyone work as hard as you have to change. Carrie will be surprised and pleased."

Elaine shook her head. "I don't know. I've disappointed her for years."

"God has begun a great work in you," Connie said, patting her arm. "He's not going to leave you now. Just ask him, and he will help you through this."

I rolled my chair to the couch, and sat in it facing the ladies. "Let's go ahead and pray now."

"Lord, let your peace fall upon Elaine and give her the help she needs. Bring her family together in your love. In Jesus' name."

Elaine took a deep breath. "Well, I'd better go upstairs and get ready. Thanks for the encouragement."

That day, Elaine's family—ravaged for years by her destructive lifestyle—would begin to heal. It didn't happen overnight, but the fruit of God's practical, relevant love initiated the healing process.

Afterward, I never had to encourage Elaine to read the Bible or pray again. She had a passion for God that moved every person crossing her path. She continued asking questions, always challenging us, always looking for a Christianity that worked in her everyday life.

We still had much to learn, but because of Elaine, our foundation at the mission was laid. With a simple, clear understanding of God's perfect love, we could offer a practical way of living for people in crisis.

# ELEVEN

## Strings Attached

Not long after Elaine's ordeal, I faced a very different kind of challenge. One I hadn't anticipated. Elaine had fixed her specialty for supper—chimichangas—and must have used every plate, pan, and utensil in the house. We declared the kitchen a disaster, but Elaine's cooking was always worth it. After the meal, Heidi stood at the kitchen sink tackling a mountain of dishes.

By this time, most of our residents had gone outside to enjoy the beautiful evening. I walked into the kitchen and couldn't believe the transformation. Floors were clean and shiny, counters had been cleared and wiped, and tables looked ready for a new day.

I strolled over to Heidi, still scrubbing on the last encrusted pot. "Wow, you did a fantastic job cleaning tonight. Everything looks great."

She stiffened, dropping the pan in the water. Covering her face with her hands, she ran past me out of the kitchen. I could hear her muffled cries going up the staircase.

Speechless, I stood there for a moment.

*Did I say something wrong?*

I told her she did a good job. What just happened?

I went upstairs to talk to her. Outside Heidi's door, I heard weeping. When I knocked, she didn't answer. I asked one of our resident ladies to check on her, thinking Heidi might talk to a woman. Heidi ignored her, too.

*What am I missing, Lord?*

Baffled, I found Elaine. She and Heidi had become close friends. If anyone could talk to her, it would be Elaine. Heidi looked up to her, taking many cues from her.

I stayed at the bottom of the stairs listening as she knocked on Heidi's door.

"It's me…Elaine," I heard her say. "Can I come in?" The door opened and closed, and then there was silence. I returned to the office to wait.

Thirty minutes later, Elaine came downstairs and planted herself in the middle of the office couch. She looked at me with raised eyebrows.

"Heidi thought you were coming on to her."

"What?" I said, stunned. "All I did was compliment her on the kitchen. You know how messy it was tonight. I just told her—"

Elaine cut in. "This has nothing to do with you, Scott. It's Heidi. She's young and she's been used by people her whole life. You said that about her yourself."

"Yes, but I didn't see this coming."

"Well, in her world, a compliment from a man means he expects something back. A favor of some kind. When you told her how great everything looked, she thought you were coming on to her like every other man in her life."

"Wow. Her reaction makes sense now. But that's terrible. No wonder she's upset."

"Heidi really likes it here and feels safe," Elaine said, "but this isn't the first time. In the past, whenever she started to relax and trust people, something would turn her world upside down. She's been waiting for the other shoe to drop any moment."

It felt like role reversal listening to Elaine, but I appreciated her insight into the homeless world.

"Tonight, when you praised her, she thought it was happening all over again. She wanted to run. I'm glad you asked me to talk to her, because I found her packing. I assured Heidi you had no intentions like that, which actually amazed her.

"Now she feels a little embarrassed. Especially after I told her you'd never hurt her like that. You'd protect her the way a father is *supposed* to protect a daughter."

Elaine smiled, looking pleased with herself.

"Thank you for that. I'm glad you've taken Heidi under your wing. She needs a friend like you who understands. It's hard for me to comprehend the world she grew up in, but I'm learning. Would you mind asking her to come downstairs? I'd like to talk about what happened before it creates a barrier between us."

"Sure." She sprang from the couch and headed upstairs.

A little while later, both came down to the office. Heidi ducked into the nearest end of the couch, curling up. Elaine, choosing the other end, looked happy to be here.

"Are you okay?"

Not looking up, Heidi gave me a weak nod. She had her arms tightly wound around her knees.

"I'm sorry about what happened earlier. Sometimes I forget how the events of your past still affect you. It's hard for me to understand because my life has been so different.

"Earlier, when I complimented you, I meant nothing more. The kitchen looked wonderful, and I wanted to say thank you for a job well done. Maybe you've noticed how poorly some people do that chore."

"Yes, I have," Elaine said, butting in. "Those ladies smear dirt all around and don't get anything clean. I have to follow up like their mother, making sure the tables and counters aren't all mucked up." She turned to Heidi. "Why don't you be the official trainer and show everyone how to clean?"

"No, thank you," she said, loosening the grip on her legs. She glanced in my direction. "I'm sorry I ran out on you like that. You scared me. I wanted to get out before you asked me to do something I didn't want to do."

"That's okay. Elaine explained it to me. I'm just sorry you had to go through that in your past."

"Nothing in my world is free. Not even nice words."

A tear fell onto her knee.

"The price is always higher than I want to pay. I really don't want to talk about it. I just wish it would all go away. Every time I think I'm doing better, a horrible memory comes back. Or something happens that makes me want to run."

"When your past sneaks up on you, Heidi, or when you feel threatened in some way, please come and talk to us about it. We're here to help you sort it out. My hope is that you'll feel comfortable enough to bring us any concerns you have."

"I would like to," she said, "but I'm not used to having people care about me. It's easier to run away than take another risk. The truth is I'm really tired of running. I don't want to do this the rest of my life."

"Well, we want to help you if you're willing. You can come to the office anytime you want to talk or ask a question."

"You mean I can ask you anything?"

"Of course."

She raised her eyes. "Even a question about your religion?"

"Absolutely. Why would Christianity be off the table?"

She straightened her legs, placing her feet on the floor.

"My father didn't teach me a whole lot, but he pounded one thing in my head: never talk about politics or religion."

"Why not?" Elaine asked.

"When I was seven or eight, I asked a guy at the bar if he believed in God. My dad almost dropped the glass he was filling. He cussed and grabbed my arm and dragged me to the back storeroom. He shoved me against a rack, yelling, 'Don't do that. You're driving away customers.' He looked so mad, I knew he'd beat me if it ever happened again. So I quit asking questions."

"That's not how it works here," I said. "You can ask us anything you want. I can't guarantee an answer, but we'll give it a try."

Just then, we heard angry twitters coming from outside the window. The three of us watched a mother robin fighting off a much bigger bird in the tree. The trespasser, having had enough, flew away. The mother robin settled down in her nest.

"All right," Heidi said, sitting straighter, mustering her own courage. "I have a question about God that has bothered me for years."

"We like to talk about God around here. What's your question?"

"When I was eleven and moved in with my second foster family, they took me to church. My foster mom told me God loves me and that his son, Jesus, loves me, too.

"It sounded really great, and I wanted to believe them, but I couldn't."

Her eyes, shiny with tears, stared into mine.

"If there's a God in heaven who really loves me, where was he when *I* was growing up? If he really cares, why would he let all those horrible things happen to me?

"Elaine told me God loves everyone and gives each of us what we need for lasting joy and peace. I really like that and wish it were true, but it doesn't make sense for *me*. *My* life was miserable and lonely. Why didn't God give me what *I* needed? Where was he when *I* needed him most?"

Seeing her tears overflow, Elaine seized the tissue box from my desk.

Most days, I would prefer to pray and ponder longer, but Heidi needed an answer now. Her question was, and still is, the king of all "why" questions, and one that requires a humble seeking of the Lord.

Any words I could offer had the potential to affect her for the rest of her life. At that moment, she needed more than a book or a theological discourse. She needed something that would soften her pain.

And I needed the wisdom of God.

*Lord, give me your thoughts. Help me answer Heidi's question.*

That instant, the doorbell rang.

"Hold on, ladies, I'll get the door." I greeted three happy women carrying cookies and a gigantic container of popcorn, freshly popped.

"We thought you folks would enjoy a snack tonight," one said, pushing the popcorn into my hands.

"Wow, thank you for thinking of us. It smells great. Would you like a receipt?"

"Oh, no, we all chipped in. It only cost pennies. Enjoy." Closing the door, I carried the snacks in. My mind was still on Heidi's question, but the sight and smell of fresh popcorn and cookies started drawing people to the kitchen, including Elaine and Heidi.

"Grab some popcorn, ladies, and we'll finish our conversation when you get back."

"Sounds good to me," Elaine said, pulling a stack of bowls out of the cabinet.

I walked back to the office, thanking God for popcorn and the extra time to pray.

# TWELVE

## River of Love

Elaine and Heidi returned, carrying heaping bowls of popcorn. "Did you ladies leave any for the rest of the house?"

"Yes, but it's going fast," Elaine said, backing herself into the couch. Heidi took her spot at the other end.

"Okay, shall we continue?"

They nodded, chewing their popcorn.

*Lord, I need your help.*

"Heidi, suppose God loves you so much, even before your conception, he placed you exactly where he wanted you here on earth.[1] What if he led you to this moment, to this exact place where you're sitting right now? Maybe the pain you view as a curse is actually a blessing from God to prepare you for something better later on."

Her mouth opened, but she waited for more.

"Imagine for a moment how your life might be different now if you'd been born into the family of your dreams. Let's say, growing up, this family cared about you and gave you everything you wanted. But instead of appreciating it, you took it for granted and became arrogant and self-serving. What if later, as an adult, you began creating more pain in the lives of others than you ever experienced yourself?"

She stopped eating and set her popcorn aside.

"Maybe God allowed you to be broken from the beginning of your life to prepare you to accept his love right now. Maybe your past was the humbling agent you needed to bring about a deep desire for a heavenly Father who wants to give you lasting joy and peace."

Elaine burst out, "That was *my* life! My family didn't go to church, but I had every material thing I could want. I wish I could say I was thankful, but I never appreciated any of it. I always wanted more. I longed to be the center of everyone's attention, especially my father's. My life became all about *me*, all about feeling good."

She turned to Heidi. "I ended up losing every single thing and every person in my life. I was never the wife, mother, or friend I should've been. I'm not saying I'd be a better person if I'd gone through all the pain you did, but I know for a fact, it's easier to deal with the pain others have inflicted on *me* than to deal with the pain I've caused *them*."

"But I didn't have a choice," Heidi said, teary-eyed. "I was born into this mess. I had to face being rejected every single day of my life. No one loved me. People took what they wanted from me and moved on.

"Now I have nothing and nobody." Her voice wavered. "Most of my days have been sad and lonely. If God really loves me, why didn't he give me a better life?"

Tears skimmed over her cheeks. Elaine moved closer, wrapping an arm around her.

*God, please help Heidi understand your love.*

"I cannot imagine what your life must feel like," I said, "but I'm convinced, no matter how terrible things are, God's love continues to flow down on you like a river, winding around and through your circumstances. Sometimes it's hard to recognize, because most people see love as being soft and gentle, like hearts and flowers.

"But God's love is deeper than that. He knows exactly what we need in this life to find lasting joy and peace. That means we might hurt for awhile, or go through hard times. Yet in this, God gives us opportunities to reach out and find him.[2]

"The question is, can we believe in a Creator God who truly loves us? Can we trust that he knows far more than we do, and continually gives us what we need?

"If we accept God's love, we can enter into the freedom of his joy and peace, drawing closer to him. If we reject his love, we can spend our whole lives looking for ways to numb our pain and disappointments, never finding real answers.

"No matter what we choose, God continues to love us, because *that's who he is*."[3]

Her eyes clouded with confusion.

"Heidi, the world you were born into rejected God's love. In fact, you were so far removed, you experienced your own personal hell here on earth. Then, after a series of scary events, you wound up on our doorstep alone.

"The day you arrived, you told us you were born homeless. After hearing your story, I have to agree, but it goes back even further. You were *conceived* homeless. By that, I mean, the circumstances surrounding your conception set you up for rejection, and you've had to live with that painful reality every day of your life."

Heidi's lip quivered.

"Now, we might wonder, why did God's love allow your mom to fall into the arms of another man instead of her husband? If God had intervened, you might not be here at all.

"But since you were born, we can ask, why did God's love allow your stepfather to reject you in the hospital? Or let your mother abandon you as an innocent baby? Why did he allow you to grow up with an alcoholic father who raised you in a bar alongside drunkards who hurt you? And why would he let others take advantage of you later?

"The questions go on and on. There are a hundred million ways God could have stepped in and changed your history. For that matter, why did God's love allow Adam and Eve to make the wrong choice in the first place? Freedom just might be overrated, you know.

"The answer is the same for all of these questions. God is love,[4] and Perfect Love cannot demand a specific response, *and still be love*. If he forces us to respond a certain way, then love is lost, and self-serving manipulation takes its place."

Her brow creased.

"Are you're saying if God loves people, he has to let them act badly and hurt others?"

"Let me put it this way," I said. "Earlier this evening, you impressed me with how well you cleaned the kitchen. I thanked you for your hard work, and triggered an avalanche of emotions from your past. You assumed I had ulterior motives, which scared you. Your fear caused you to reject my simple expression of gratitude. You ran to your room and locked the door."

She flushed, remembering.

"What would you have done if I'd grabbed your arm on your way past me, forcing you to stop and accept my compliment?"

"My fear would turn to anger, and I'd fight to get away. You'd never see me again."

"So forcing you to do what *I* wanted would've been the worst possible thing for you at that moment?"

"Yes, it would be awful. I'd feel trapped."

"Okay, in the same way, if God forces us to respond *his* way, we'd also feel trapped. And love would be lost.

"From the time of your conception, Heidi, I believe God has used the circumstances of your life to bring you to this place, this moment, to give you an opportunity to either accept his love or reject it."

I stretched back in my chair, quiet. I knew the concept of a loving God lay outside her known world.

Elaine took this opportunity for refills. "Can I get anyone a bowl of popcorn or something?"

"Sure," I said. "I'll take a cookie if there's any left."

"Just water for me," Heidi said.

When Elaine returned, I began to wrap up our conversation. I didn't want to overwhelm Heidi.

"Well, what do you think?" I asked her. "Can you believe there's a Father in heaven who loves you even though he's allowed pain in your life?"

Her eyes became misty.

"I'd like to," she said, "but I don't know how to trust anyone yet. Not even God."

"That's understandable—you've been hurt by many people. Why don't you take the next few weeks to think about your life, what you want to change, and what you hope to see in your future? You can take your time. There's no hurry."

Relaxing, she scooped a handful of popcorn.

"Thank you for listening to me," she said. "I'm really glad you didn't get mad when I asked you about God. I've always wanted to believe in him. I just didn't know much about him. I will think about what you said today. I hope I can learn to trust God the way you all do."

"No pressure at all. Feel free to come back and talk. We have an open-door policy here."

The ladies collected their dishes and made their way to the door. Elaine, following Heidi, looked back and winked, giving me a thumbs-up.

Whew.

*Thank you, Lord, for giving me your words.*

# THIRTEEN

## Gone Too Soon

A month after our conversation, Heidi showed up in our office doorway, glowing. "I'm ready to accept God's love," she announced. Connie and Elaine, sitting on the couch, stopped talking and stared at her. Heidi's bold declaration surprised all of us.

I motioned for her to come in.

"I've been thinking about this a lot," she said, sitting in a rocking chair in the corner, a recent gift from one of our volunteers. "I want a Father in my life who loves me and I want Jesus to be my savior. I've done some really dumb things in my life, and I want Jesus to forgive me.

"I also need him to help me live a better life. I'm not doing very well on my own."

Connie handed her a tissue.

"I would've told you about my decision earlier," she said, wiping her eyes, "but the idea of getting baptized scared me. After fretting a few days, I finally thought, what do I have to lose?"

"Nothing, if you ask me," Elaine said. "I'll be there and make sure you don't drown."

Heidi chuckled.

"So if it's all right with everyone," she said, "I'd like to accept Jesus and start my new life today."

We were thrilled, of course, but I wanted to make sure she wasn't doing this for us or anyone else. We asked her a few questions, and by the time we finished our conversation, she had won us over with her answers. She genuinely desired a new way of life.

That afternoon, we prayed with Heidi and loaded up the mission van with our residents and staff. We drove across town to South Side Christian Church where I baptized her.

When Heidi came out of the water, she heard loud singing, clapping, and cheering—a wonderful welcome into the kingdom of God.

"For the first time, I know what peace feels like," she told us later. "I don't feel scared or alone anymore."

During the next few weeks, we saw positive changes taking place in her life. From the moment she accepted God's love, Heidi began to flourish. Like Elaine, she found great joy in reading the Bible. "God is talking to *me*!" she exclaimed.

We hoped this newfound joy would help her build a new life. She had lots of enthusiasm and a desire to learn. All she needed was more time.

The following week, Heidi overheard me telling a mother with a young daughter we didn't have a room available. Afterward, she came into the office with a somber face. She perched on the arm of the loveseat.

"Scott, I don't want to be the reason someone's child is on the street. Maybe I should move in with my mom today. Those people need my room."

"Your mom?"

"Not my bio mom—my foster mom, the second one. She still cares about me, and we talk on the phone sometimes."

"Does she know you're here?"

"She does now. I called her the other day, and she was really happy to hear from me. We hadn't talked for almost a year. She said if I ever need a place to stay, I can move in with her family again. They only have two kids at home now and an extra room. I told her I planned on staying here longer, but after hearing you turn down that mother, I think I should go ahead and move out."

"That's a nice offer, Heidi, but don't rush this. After living with your father, you've rarely stayed anywhere more than a year. You have a better chance of success if you wait until you're ready. We used to send people off too soon, thinking they could handle the pressures of life. Now we know that doesn't work. Why don't you slow down and try to learn as much as you can here? You don't want to end up homeless again."

Weighing the idea, she agreed. "Okay, maybe you're right. I just hate seeing mothers and children with no place to go. Especially now that I'm doing better."

"I understand, and that's one of the hardest parts of our job. We don't like turning anyone away. But we've learned to trust God and his timing. He brings the right people at the right time."

In the days following our conversation, Heidi began spending time at her foster mom's house. She spent a night there, then a weekend. We watched their growing bond.

Then one day Heidi showed up at our office doorway, peering through the upper half of the double door. We had closed the bottom half to keep small children from wandering in and out. "Can we talk?" she asked.

Connie waved her in, sliding over on the couch. "How are things going?"

"Well, that's why I'm here." She closed the door and plopped down next to Connie. "I think I'm ready to move in with my foster mom now. We get along great and have so much in common."

Her eyes shone with excitement.

I pushed my paperwork aside. "I hope that doesn't change. You know from past experience, things aren't always the way they appear at first."

"Yeah, but this is different. I can tell she really loves me. I want to give her a chance. I need a mom in my life."

"It may seem like the perfect opportunity right now," Connie said, "but after everything you've been through, I hope it isn't too soon. You're a great person and your foster mom sees that, but things are different now."

"What do you mean?"

"You've suffered a lot of pain and rejection. You aren't that eleven year old being taken care of anymore. You began pushing back at life and started taking control. You stopped trusting people."

Heidi blinked back tears.

"And the decisions you made led you into chaos," I said. "You're doing great now and that's wonderful, but I believe you need more time. If you stay, we can help you learn how to make better decisions with your life."

"But my foster mom really cares about me," she said. "Don't you think moving in with her is a good decision? She can help me do better."

"I'm just saying if you leave now, it's not going to be an easy road for you. That's why I encouraged you to stay here longer when you asked to move out earlier."

"But my life has never been easy. I'm just glad I have a mom who cares about me. I can at least try and make it work, don't you think? I've already told her I'm moving in with them."

I felt a pit in my stomach. I knew we had to let her go.

"You have to do what you feel is best," Connie said. "Your foster mom will be blessed to have you. Just remember, when life gets hard—and it will—God still loves you. He'll be there no matter what."

Heidi moved closer, giving Connie a hug.

"I won't forget," she said. "I still want a Father in my life."

She came over and hugged me, too.

"Are you moving out today?" I asked.

She gave me an apologetic nod. "They're getting my room ready now."

I tried to sound upbeat. "Well, I hope you stop by or call sometime. We'd like to know how you're doing. Please let us know if you ever need anything."

"I will," she said, stepping into the doorway. She turned to face us.

"Yes, we would love to see you again," Connie said, with tears in her eyes, "and so would Miss Daisy. Remember, you can always come back for our Bible studies and classes."

"I'd like to."

She lingered for a moment. "I guess this is goodbye then."

I managed a smile. "Stay close to God. Accept his love and enjoy your new life."

"I will," she said with watery eyes. "Thank you for everything. I'd better go and get my stuff packed. I didn't know this would be so hard."

Heidi ran up the stairs, and Connie and I reflected over the changes in her life. When she first arrived on our porch a few months earlier, she only had the clothes on her back. Now she would leave with two full suitcases and a bag. More than that, she would leave with a heavenly Father who loved her dearly.

That thought comforted us as we mulled her decision to move out.

An hour later, saying our final goodbyes on the front porch, Connie and I felt a loss. Would we ever see her again? Heidi wasn't the first person to leave the mission too early. We wanted to protect her and keep her with us longer. But we couldn't.

*Lord, please take care of her.*

We wouldn't hear from Heidi for almost twenty years. It wasn't until a friend of ours met her in his small home town several hours away that we had a chance to reconnect.

Talking with Heidi, we found out her life had taken many turns, both good and bad. Yet, amidst her joys and sorrows, she never lost her love for God. We told Heidi she'd made a difference in our world, and she was thrilled. Later, we asked if we could use her story to help others, and she was ecstatic. She couldn't wait to share the news with her children.

"I've always hoped God would bring good out of my life," she said, with tears. "Now I can tell my kids God really *does* care, and he turns our worst things into something good."

The day Heidi moved out of the mission those twenty years earlier, she'd left us with a gift. She had opened a window into her broken world, giving us one more piece in the puzzle of homelessness.

# FOURTEEN

## The Birthday Party

Elaine's path looked much different than Heidi's. At thirty-eight years of age, she'd spent half of her life using drugs and alcohol before coming to the mission.

She would stay with us much longer than Heidi. Now, more than a year after her arrival, she was still growing and changing.

"I wish I'd learned all this sooner," she told us one morning after breakfast. "Because of my selfish decisions, my daughters are now stuck with their own haunting memories to deal with."

Elaine pulled out a tissue, dabbing her eyes.

I set my coffee mug on the desk and leaned back. "It's not easy watching your children live with decisions you made years ago, but you're a different person today. And now that you're clean and sober, you can help your daughters through *their* difficult times, which you couldn't do before."

"I suppose so. I just wish they didn't grow up with my stupidity."

"You're at a better place now," Connie said, rocking our seven-month old son, Isaac, the newest member of our family. "Many good things are happening. People see how you've changed, and they want you back in their lives."

"That's true," I said. "Youth ministers wouldn't invite you to speak at their events if you didn't inspire their teens and sponsors. Your testimony motivates many people, including our residents and staff."

"You have a passion most people wish they had," Connie said. "Haven't you noticed how volunteer groups gather around *you* when they come to the mission? They want to see life through *your* eyes. You inspire them."

Elaine, taking this in, dried more tears. She tossed her tissue in the trash. "Thank you. I do see God putting my life back together. It's slower than I want, but I *am* a different person than I was last year. And, yes, I've noticed people hanging around me. I thought it was because of my good looks."

She let out a hoot, making us all laugh.

"Well, if I've helped even one person, maybe God can use me after all my years of stupidity."

"He already has," I said. "God is opening doors for you in ways you've never dreamed possible. I'm excited to see what he has in store for you next."

"And you're getting custody of your daughter," Connie said. "That's pretty awesome, don't you think?"

"I can't believe I'm getting a second chance with Kimi. I'm delighted, of course, but scared to death. I've never raised a child *sober*. I'm going to need lots of advice."

"We're here for you," I said.

Checking the clock, Elaine sprang to her feet. "Kimi's moving in on Saturday, and I need to get the sheets washed. I'm giving her the top bunk—I'm not as limber as I used to be."

"None of us are," I said, chuckling.

Elaine spent the next two days moving her belongings to a bigger room and getting it ready for Kimi. The fear of raising her sixth grade daughter would overtake her at times, bringing her down to the office.

"You can do this," we told her more than once. "We're here if anything happens."

On Saturday, her daughter moved in and we watched their new life begin. Kimi, seeing positive changes in her mother, settled right in, happy to be reunited.

Two days later, Elaine raced downstairs to the office.

"I need to find a steady job," she told us, out of breath. "I have to prepare for our future and save money for a house."

Since coming off house restriction ten months earlier, Elaine had only worked temporary jobs. We had encouraged her to re-enter the workplace slowly—and she willingly did—but now she felt ready to tackle full-time employment. "I'll have plenty of time while Kimi attends school," she explained.

We gave her our blessing.

Later that day, Elaine reconnected with an old friend, a previous co-worker who had started her own business. The woman, remembering Elaine's cooking skills, offered her a full-time position as a cook and caterer. Elaine now had a consistent way to earn and save money.

A week into her new job, she came down to the office again.

"I'm not worried about using anymore," she said, standing at the desk. "I think I'm finally moving past that. I don't have time to focus on my old cravings anyway. I have a daughter to care for and relationships to work on. Most are doing great, except I still have trouble with Kimi's dad."

"What kind of trouble?" I asked.

"Sam doesn't trust the changes in my life. He says he's not fooled by my turnaround or my 'new faith.' He's watched me hurt Kimi too many times in the past. I hope I can prove him wrong. I'm trying to apply Christian love and give him what he needs. I've talked with the staff here and they've given me lots of pointers."

A proud smile went across her face.

"I've been learning to use fewer words with him and follow through on what I say. I've also stopped making promises. That always gets me into trouble."

"You sound like a much wiser person," I said, thrilled at the news.

"Well, I should be. I've had tons of help. No matter what Sam thinks, I'm happy to say I've been clean and sober thirteen months."

I gave her a high five. "You've come a long way, Elaine. We should celebrate."

She stepped back, dropping on the couch.

"Speaking of celebration, Scott, I have a question. Kimi's turning twelve next month and I'm wondering if I can throw a surprise birthday party for her. A big one. I want to make up for all the birthdays I missed in the past."

I sat back in my chair. "I'm listening."

"My boss said I could have it at our workplace. She has a huge room for catered parties and told me I could invite as many people as I wanted. I'd like you and your family to come. I already have most of it planned in my head. I even found a DJ with a karaoke machine."

"Sounds like a blow-out. Can you handle the cost?"

"I think so. I'm getting the room for free and my boss is giving me a discount on food. I can bake the cakes myself, make sandwiches, and buy a few decorations. I'm hoping Sam will cover the DJ cost. We may not see eye-to-eye, but he'll do anything for our daughter."

"Sounds like the perfect party. I'm sure my family would love to come. Just don't stress over it. You're doing great now."

She bounded from the couch, hugging me. "Oh, I won't. Carrie wants to help. I'm so excited."

In the weeks leading up to the party, Elaine spent time finalizing every detail. Her enthusiasm spilled onto everyone at the mission. She hoped to make Kimi's birthday party an event she'd never forget. And we all wanted to help.

When the big day finally came, Connie and I arrived early to help Elaine get ready. Carrie and several of our staff members had already set up the tables. We decorated the room with balloons and streamers, and others arranged food on the trays. After that, we set out pictures of Kimi and sprinkled confetti on the tables. Finishing up, we all made a final inspection and agreed the room looked festive and ready for Kimi's big party.

Elaine checked her watch. "I need to go back to the mission and get dressed. I've been here since eight o'clock this morning."

"Sounds good," I said. "I'll stay here and greet the early arrivals as we planned."

Carrie walked over. "Mom, you have ninety minutes until Kimi gets here with Sam. Please don't be late."

Elaine held up her car keys, jingling them. She'd been blessed with a "like-new" car from one of our volunteer groups. "Oh, I'll be back in plenty of time," she said, sashaying toward the exit. "I have my own wheels now."

On her way out, we heard her singing, "On the Road Again,"[1] in a southern twang.

Soon after, Connie left to go pick up our children. Elaine had asked everyone to arrive early for the surprise party, so our family would have to be here at least ten minutes before six o'clock—the time Sam planned to walk in with Kimi.

At five-thirty, the guests started arriving. We took turns

ushering them into the big party room. Within twenty minutes, the whole room was packed with people and presents. We turned out the lights at five-fifty and waited together in silence. Connie and I leaned against the back wall with our children, hushing them as best we could.

With five minutes to go, Connie whispered, "I haven't seen Elaine. I hope she's around here somewhere."

I glanced around. "I'm sure she's on the property. She wouldn't be late for this."

At six o'clock, right on schedule, Kimi walked through the door with her father. The lights flashed on and the whole room yelled, "Surprise!" with people blowing on kazoos and singing, "Happy Birthday."

"We love you, Kimi," several hollered.

She looked around, her eyes shining. "You all came here for me? I can't believe it. I've never had a surprise party before." People gathered around, giving her hugs.

Kimi beamed, saying, "Thank you so much," as she greeted them.

Not seeing her mother anywhere, I said to Connie, "I'm going to check around. I'll be right back."

*Lord, help Elaine show up before Kimi notices.*

I searched all over, even the back parking lot. No Elaine. I returned to the party in time to see Sam grabbing the karaoke mike. I walked over to Connie.

"Sam's taking over as party host," she explained. "He doesn't seem at all surprised Elaine didn't show."

We saw Kimi standing in the middle of the room, scanning faces. It would only be a matter of seconds. My heart weighed heavy for her. I'll never forget the look of confusion and hurt on her face when she didn't find her mother in the crowd.

"Do you think she'll come?" Connie asked.

"I don't know why she wouldn't."

The party lasted two hours. We listened to music, ate great food, and watched Kimi open presents. Soon, bad karaoke filled the room, making us all laugh. Everyone stayed upbeat for Kimi's sake. No one talked about her mother. Carrie just shrugged when I looked at her.

Some of us stayed afterward to clean up. Kimi's friends kept her busy until we finished. She laughed and sounded cheerful, but I could see the pain in her eyes.

"Are you taking Kimi home with you tonight?" I asked, hoping her dad had thought of that.

"Yeah, I'll take her," Sam said, shaking his head. "This isn't the first birthday party her mother missed. I thought she put this stuff behind her."

"We did too."

None of us heard a word from Elaine that night.

# FIFTEEN

## Ghosts of the Past

At home the next morning, my first thought getting out of bed was Elaine. *Has anyone heard from her?* Scenarios flashed through my mind as I ate breakfast with my family, and I decided to make a few calls.

I reached for the phone, but it rang first, making me jump.

"Scott?"

"Yes, it's me."

"Mom's in the hospital. She overdosed on crack and sleeping pills last night." I recognized Carrie's voice. "They had to pump her stomach."

"Is she okay?"

"I think so, but the doctor said she almost didn't make it. Her body's wearing out."

Carrie exhaled a deep sigh.

"Right now, she can't talk. Her vocal cords are damaged. The doc told us her voice will come back in a day or two. He thinks she'll sleep most of that time anyway."

"How are you holding up?"

"Fine, I suppose. I just wish this would stop. Mom's been doing so much better—" Carrie's voice cracked. "She's been clean more than a year now. She started over."

"Don't give up on her, Carrie. I'll drop by the hospital this afternoon."

Standing in her doorway, I saw Elaine lying motionless in her hospital bed. I knocked before entering her room. Carrie, sitting in a nearby recliner, looked exhausted. I signaled for her to stay seated.

"Hey, Scott," she said, with a tired smile.

Elaine stirred, opening her eyes. Struggling to sit up and talk, she fell back on her pillow, weeping.

I held my hand up. "No need to talk now. I'm only staying a few minutes. We'll talk later when you return to the mission."

She wept harder.

"Mom didn't know if you'd let her come back," Carrie said.

"She can."

Standing at Elaine's side, I took her hand.

"Elaine, the overdose almost killed you. Your body can't take this anymore. This might be your last chance. You need to decide whether you want to live or die."

Tears rolled down her swollen face.

I said a quick prayer: "Lord, thank you for giving Elaine another chance. Help her to use her life for your glory. In Jesus' name."

Two days later, the hospital released her. At the mission, I only saw a glimpse of her climbing the stairs to her room. She shut the door and slept for another two days.

When Elaine finally came downstairs, she stood in the office doorway looking pale, but better.

"Can I come in?" she asked.

I waved toward the couch. She crept across the room and slumped into it. I waited for her to speak.

"Well, I have no excuses to offer," she mumbled, staring at the floor. "I let everyone down, especially Kimi. She may never forgive me. I'm starting to wonder if this is who I am."

I pushed the keyboard away and studied her for a moment. She cautiously lifted her eyes.

"Well, are you going to say anything?"

In our silence, she twisted a lock of her limp, red-brown hair.

"Yes," I finally said. "Stop feeling sorry for yourself. Kimi will forgive you in time. I agree you messed up and almost got yourself killed, but you're still ahead of where you were last year. You've taken hundreds of steps forward, and now one step back. I know it seems like a big step, but it doesn't have to be. You can learn from this and move on."

"How?" she asked, wide-eyed.

"Forgive yourself. God knew you were going to mess up long before you did. The Bible says Jesus knew Peter would deny him three times.[1] In the same way, God knew you weren't going to show up for Kimi's party. He also knew you'd be sorry. And like Peter, you can learn a life lesson from this and change."

"I keep asking God to forgive me," she said, her eyes welling up.

"Well, he has. Now, assess the damage and start picking up the pieces. You may be surprised at how much you still have intact. Do you still want to move forward? Or do you want to give up and go back to your old life?"

Tears ran down her cheeks. I tossed her the box of tissues.

"I want to move forward, I really do," she said in a lackluster tone. "My life was going great until Kimi's birthday party."

"Okay, I have a question for you. Something I've wondered since visiting you at the hospital."

She dried her eyes, focusing.

"What was the last thing you thought about before using Friday night? What went through your mind?"

"Oh, that's easy. The parties."

"What parties?"

"The birthday parties my dad paid for, but never bothered to attend." Her voice quavered. "I wasn't important enough. He couldn't waste his time on me."

Elaine bowed her head and wept. I rolled my chair around to the front of the couch and waited.

When her tears slowed, she lifted her bloodshot eyes.

"I didn't know Kimi's twelfth birthday party would bring back all those old feelings. They still haunt me. I'm so ashamed of myself. Do you think I'll ever stop using?"

I reclined in my chair.

*Lord, I need your direction.*

Seconds later, a childhood memory, one I hadn't thought about in years, came to mind.

"Let me tell you a story," I said. "When I was Kimi's age, I lived four blocks from a basketball court in my small hometown. It had become a favorite gathering spot for all the boys in town. That year, on my twelfth birthday, my parents gave me an orange rubber basketball, and I couldn't wait to try it out. The next day, I proudly carried it to the court.

"Seeing my rubber ball, a high school boy started pointing and laughing, saying, 'Look at the baby toy.' He grabbed it and kicked it down the road almost two blocks. I ran as fast as I could, chasing it, hoping my new ball wasn't lost. Finally, I caught up with it and carried it back to the court, thinking the boy might leave me alone.

"Well, as soon as he saw me, he ran over and kicked my ball even farther down the road. Once again, I chased after it, but this time when I came back, I carried it to a different hoop on the court, hoping the boy would forget about me. Instead, he rushed over and swiped my ball mid-air.

"I waited, fully expecting to see my new ball plummeting down the road again. But then a different boy—a starter on the high school basketball team—stepped in and grabbed it. I heard him say, 'Leave the kid alone. He's not hurting anyone.'

"Next, he handed it to me, saying, 'You have a nice ball, kid. Shoot over there at the far end of the court, so you don't get hurt.' And he walked away.

"Later that day at home, I told my mom what happened. She listened, but didn't say a word about the kid making fun of me. She only asked me one question: 'When you grow up, Scott, which boy do you want to be like?'"

I looked at Elaine, who still had tears trickling down.

"You feel terrible because of the way your father treated you. Why would you want to act like your father and treat your daughter the same way?"

Her eyes opened wide.

"For the past year, you've experienced the love of a heavenly Father. Now, ask yourself, which one do you want to be like?

"How much longer will you use your earthly father to justify your addictions? Isn't it time you take responsibility for your own actions? You have daughters and friends who love you and need you. *They're* here for you now. Isn't that something to celebrate?"

She gave me a feeble nod.

"Last week, we studied Philippians in the lodge living room. In chapter four, Paul talks about rejoicing in the Lord always, being thankful in everything. He says to focus on good things, which allow the God of peace to dwell inside of you.[2]

"Elaine, you've already felt the God of peace in your life. He's healed you in many ways. Let him finish the good work he's started in you. Focus on your blessings. Mimic the good behavior you see in caring people around you. If you do, you'll destroy the ghosts of your past."

Tears flooded her eyes, sliding down.

"Romans 8:38 says nothing can separate you from the love of God. Nothing. Not death nor life, not angels nor demons, not the present nor the future. Nothing in all creation.[3]

"If you focus on your blessings, I believe you will never use again."

She swabbed her cheeks with a clump of tissues.

"You really think so?"

"Yes, I do. Now is the time to enjoy each day God gives you. Celebrate the love you've found in him. Rejoice in the love you give and receive from others."

"Scott, will you say a prayer for me?"

"I'd be happy to.

"Lord, help Elaine see what *you* see. In Jesus' name."

Afterward, she groaned. "Oh no, I just remembered. I'm supposed to give my testimony at the Lincoln youth group Sunday night. How can I go now, after my huge mess-up?"

"Show up and be honest," I said. "Tell them what happened. See how they respond. You might be surprised."

"Oh, I can't do that. I'm not strong enough."

I laughed long and hard.

She gawked at me.

"When it comes to frankness," I said, "you have reserves of steel. Tell the kids the truth. Think it over and let me know in the morning."

Sighing, she trudged out of the office.

# SIXTEEN

## Free at Last

The next morning on Saturday, Elaine walked into the office. "I've decided to give my testimony," she said, gazing across the desk at me. "Someone may need to hear about God's love, how he never gives up on us, even when we give up on ourselves. I will go for that one person."

"I'm happy to hear that."

"I'm hoping Sam will let Kimi come with me. She loves the Lincoln youth group and has made friends with some of the girls. Can I call him?"

"Line one is yours," I said, pushing a button. I hoped Sam would let his daughter go. Twice a month, the Lincoln Christian Church would bring a busload of high schoolers to the mission to lead a worship service and hang out with our residents. Kimi always looked forward to their visits.

Elaine returned to the office doorway looking glum. "He didn't pick up the phone."

Sunday afternoon, Elaine rushed into the office. "Guess what? Sam's dropping Kimi off in an hour. He called me back saying he's giving me another chance. He's noticed a change in Kimi's behavior and thinks it's because of me. He said if I get my act together, she can move back in with me full time."

Tears flowed down her cheeks.

"Sam thinks she needs me. I'm so happy."

"Well, I hope you don't take his forgiveness for granted," I said. "You may not get another chance."

"Believe me, I won't. Before the doctor released me from the hospital, he said my life will be cut short because of my drug use. He doesn't know by how much, but I plan on taking advantage of every day God gives me. I want to live my life like that nice boy you talked about, Scott. I'm going to love Kimi the way my heavenly Father loves me."

That evening at the Lincoln Christian Church, Elaine stepped up to the podium. Kimi had joined her friends on the front row, while Connie and I chose seats near the back with our children.

Elaine adjusted the mike to speak.

Her voice, full of raw emotion, pierced the air. Starting with childhood, she talked about her father, how his absence shaped every decision she made for years. "I felt insignificant and angry," she told the audience, "and I had a constant desire for attention."

That led her on a lifelong search for love, she explained. The pursuit of a dream no person could fill.

With tears, she shared her journey through alcohol and drugs, saying, "I became an addict in every sense of the word, hurting every person close to me."

She talked about the money she spent, the friends she bought, and how nothing ever seemed to last. "I had a front row seat on a freight train—my life—and it was rolling down a mountain, out of control."

Tears poured down her cheeks. "I didn't know how to stop it."

Instead of facing it, Elaine clung to hope and more drugs, while exchanging one wrong man for the next.

Her life crashed, she admitted, the day she stood on our sidewalk in front of the mission more than a year earlier. She'd lost every friend and relative in the world, including her daughters.

"It was the hardest day of my life," she said, through tears. "For the first time, I realized I'd wasted almost two decades. Years I would never get back."

Elaine pulled out tissues, drying her cheeks. Looking around the room, she smiled for the first time.

"I have good news to tell you. I met someone who gives me great joy and peace."

Her voice, filled with passion, described a Father in heaven who loved her, who started putting her pieces back together. "I have my daughters back," she said, "and I have so much hope for the future. God has changed everything in my..."

Her words trailed off, and she lowered her head.

*Lord, help her finish this.*

Grasping the podium, Elaine raised her eyes.

"Well, not everything," she said quietly. "I still have ghosts from my past." With her voice trembling, she went on to confess her biggest shame: Kimi's twelfth birthday party.

"I only thought about *me*. My own pain. I forgot all about *hers*. That night, I abandoned my daughter for a high that never lasts and almost got myself killed.

"I'm so ashamed."

Throughout her testimony, her tears flowed. Especially at the end when she talked about God's love and mercy. "He never gives up on a person, ever," she said, struggling for composure. "I'm proof of that."

She backed away from the mike, finished.

The room sat still.

Taking a look around, I saw people wiping their eyes. A young girl about fourteen stood and clapped. We all joined her. We clapped for Elaine's bravery. We clapped for a Father in heaven who is merciful and forgiving. We clapped for love.

The youth minister, Jeff, a compassionate man who would later work at the mission, joined Elaine behind the podium. "Thank you for being honest," he said, wrapping an arm around her shoulders. "I know that wasn't easy."

Elaine, shedding tears, scoured her face with crumpled tissues.

"Everyone, come to the front," he called out. "Let's gather around Elaine and ask God to heal her painful memories. Ask him to take away her addictions and remove her shame and guilt. Then we'll pray for God to give her strength to continue."

Teens and sponsors walked forward, forming a perimeter around Elaine. Some laid hands on her shoulders, and others just prayed, taking turns. Afterward, Jeff closed with this prayer:

"Heavenly Father, thank you for the courage Elaine showed tonight. Thank you for setting her free from the ghosts of her past. In Jesus' name."

After Kimi's birthday party, Elaine never touched alcohol or drugs again. Within six months, she and her daughter moved into a place of their own, not far from Springfield. Elaine found employment as a baker in a small grocery store five blocks from their small duplex.

She stayed in touch with the mission, often bringing items we use most, like meat, coffee, or paper goods. Elaine considered all of us her extended family. With great pleasure, we watched her provide a steady, safe environment for Kimi, becoming the mother she always hoped she could be.

About eighteen months after their departure, I called Elaine one day, asking her to stop by the mission. Connie and I had something we wanted to give her. Awaiting her arrival, we sat in a glider on the front porch of the lodge enjoying the nice weather. We saw her car pulling up, and we walked down the sidewalk to greet her.

When we came together, we all stood on the same spot Elaine had found herself three years earlier. Connie reached into her pocket, and held out her hand. A key lay in her palm.

"What's this?" Elaine asked, bending closer.

Connie, acting nonchalant, said, "Oh, just a key."

"A key to what?"

"It's a key to your new job as lodge supervisor."

Elaine's mouth dropped open. She fixed her eyes on me. "Is she kidding?"

I chuckled. "Nope, it's for real."

Elaine lunged forward, grabbing both of us.

"Whoa," I said, catching Connie before she fell backward. "I guess this means you're happy about your new job?"

"Yes, yes, yes." She hopped around in a circle. "I didn't think this would ever happen."

"Why not? You ask for a job every time you visit."

"I didn't think you'd ever say yes."

Laughing, Connie and I gave her a hug.

"You've come a long way, Elaine. We want you to be a part of our staff."

"Yes," Connie said, patting her. "We want you to share your life with our residents and teach them what you've learned. You can help others find the same freedom you've found."

Elaine whooped loud enough for the whole block to hear.

Later that day she gave her notice at the grocery store. Two weeks after that, she joined our staff as an official lodge supervisor.

In her new job, we never had to ask Elaine to share her life with our residents. She offered her story of brokenness and pain at every opportunity, always ending with God's perfect love and forgiveness.

We felt privileged to have Elaine join our staff. Her journey and passion for God inspired countless people to change their lives. And they could always depend on Elaine to be their biggest cheerleader.

Not long after this, God would bring more people into our lives. He had more he wanted to teach us.

Only next time, our lesson came through pain.

My pain.

# SEVENTEEN

## Wasteland of Stupidity

The door of a station wagon flew open, and a boy about my son's age jumped out and ran toward the basketball hoop behind the mission. "Hey, can I shoot a few?" he yelled to Josh, my thirteen year-old, now lofting a ball in the air. I had brought Josh with me that summer day to help with donations and errands. He enjoyed shooting baskets during his down time.

I had just closed the door to the small storage shed behind the lodge and was now carrying three jumbo-sized packages of toilet paper in my arms. Walking toward the front porch, I could hear the boys' short conversation.

"Sure, you can play," Josh said, happy to have someone join him on the old concrete slab. "I'm Josh. What's your name?"

"Danny." He caught the ball, dribbling it. Like most boys their age, a name was all they needed to play ball. Josh didn't notice Danny's tattered clothes or the beat-up station wagon in the alley, filled with the kind of stuff most of us would drop off in a dumpster.

That moment, that afternoon, they were just two boys playing basketball.

I deposited the toilet paper on the front porch and headed back to the shed for more supplies.

On my way, I noticed a weary-looking woman emerging from the station wagon. She reached into her car, pulling out a large assortment of plastic grocery bags, all filled and overflowing. She placed them on the ground with great care. One by one, she hung the bags on her arms.

I opened the shed again, taking out a crate of cleaning supplies. Crimping the old padlock, I saw the woman yanking something from the back of her station wagon. A huge garbage bag fell at her feet. Locking her car, she plodded toward our shelter, dragging the bulging bag behind her.

"Is that your mom?" I heard Josh ask Danny.

"Yeah."

"She looks tired. Should we help her?"

"Nah, she's okay." Danny charged the basket for a lay-up. "Mom knows I hate moving around. Last week, I dropped one of her bags and broke a clock. Now, she won't let me carry anything."

The boys continued their game, forgetting about Danny's mother.

I carried the crate to the front porch, leaving it. I turned back toward the woman, who was now hunched forward and breathing hard. Although hot and sunny outside, the woman's long, graying hair cascaded over many layers of clothing and the bags hanging from her body.

"Can I help you carry your bags?" I asked her.

Not looking up, she released her grip on the garbage bag, leaving it behind her on the grass. "Just the big one," she said, still plodding along. I picked up the bag and followed her.

With great effort, she climbed the three steps to our front porch and waited at the top. I stepped up alongside her, opening the front door.

"Is this a shelter?" she asked, squinting in the sun.

"Yes it is. Come on in." I moved back, letting her enter first. "The office is on the left. Feel free to go in and sit on the couch."

The woman lumbered into the building and traipsed wearily into the office. She dropped her full weight, bags and all, onto the couch. Hearing her labored breaths, I decided to give her a moment.

"I'll be right back."

I brought in the crate and toilet paper, hauling them to the back supply closet. Then I found an intake packet and left it on the desk.

"Can I get you something to drink before we start?"

"Water," she said in a parched voice.

I went to the kitchen and came back with a large plastic cup of ice water. She took it from me without looking up.

I rolled my chair forward, sitting behind the desk.

"My name is Scott. How can I help you?"

Gulping her water, she emptied the cup and tossed it aside.

"I'm Darlene and my son, Danny, is outside playing ball with some kid. We need a place to stay tonight. My back is killing me."

That didn't surprise me.

"My Danny's twelve and a half. He's a good boy and won't give you any trouble."

"We had a room open up earlier today. You and your son are welcome to stay in it. I hope you don't mind bunk beds."

"We've had worse," she said, with a grunt. "I just need to stretch out." Beads of sweat rolled down her temples.

I opened the intake packet. "Okay, let's get started."

Darlene settled into the couch, relaxing. She answered my intake questions between gaping yawns, using as few words as possible. Before long, I noticed her eyes glazing over. I wondered if she'd heard any of our house guidelines. Afterward, she signed our forms without comment.

"Welcome to the mission," I said, in a cheery voice. "Let me carry your large bag for you." I led Darlene to her room in the basement, and pointed out a few necessities. Then I gave her the key and returned to the office. I figured we could talk more after she rested.

At the desk, I laid out my paperwork, ready to enter stats into the computer. Without warning, the office door flew open, bouncing against the wall. Startled, I looked up to see Danny stepping into the room. He planted his feet apart like a cowboy in a gun fight and pointed his finger at me.

"Are you Josh's father?"

"Yes, I am," I said, wondering what my son did now. We had nicknamed him Doctor Destructo years ago for his innate ability to break things. Like Bam-Bam, he was far too strong for his own good.

"Are you married to Josh's mother?"

"Yes, I'm Josh's father, and I'm married to Josh's mother."

"And he has three brothers and two sisters?"

"That's right. We have six children. Josh is our second oldest."

"So you're telling me that you and your wife have six kids and they have *no* other moms or dads?"

Danny scowled in disbelief.

"Yes, that is correct."

He didn't move, absorbing the news. Without a word, his shoulders dropped. As he turned to leave, a huge tear rolled down his face.

"What's the matter?

"Danny?"

He hurried out. At the same time, Josh came bounding through the doorway, passing him.

"What just happened, Josh? What's wrong with Danny?"

"I don't know, Dad. We were outside shooting baskets, and we got into an argument over—"

I cut in. "Josh, why do you have to be so competitive? It's just a game. You don't know anything about this boy's life. You don't always have to win."

I thought about the trivial foul or missed shot.

"Dad, we didn't fight about the game."

"Good," I said, still concerned. Connie and I had been teaching our children compassion, how to rise above the minor rifts in life—especially at the mission—but they still needed reminding.

"So why is Danny upset? What did you fight about?"

"He asked me how many brothers and sisters I had. I told him five. Then he asked me how many moms and dads I had. I told him one mom and one dad. He called me a liar. He said he was twelve years old and had never met anyone with a family like ours with only one mom and one dad."

I felt myself being pulled, once again, into a world vastly different from mine.

"Oh, Josh, I'm sorry for not listening to you before I jumped in."

"That's all right, Dad. No big deal." He looked relieved. "I came in to see if Danny was okay. He's going to be okay, isn't he?"

"I don't know, son. I hope so."

"Can I go and see if he wants to shoot more baskets?"

I nodded and he left.

Deflated, I slumped in my chair.

How could a twelve year old child never meet an intact family like ours? The look on Danny's face when he recognized for the first time *what he never had* broke my heart.

Before I could dwell on the subject, a waft of cigarette smoke floated into the office. I would have to go find the source. Following the trail, I found myself standing outside Darlene's room in the basement. Clearly, she missed my no-smoking spiel earlier. I knocked on her door. Hearing no response, I knocked again.

"Darlene, are you smoking in your room?"

"Yes, I am. Is there a problem?"

"I'm afraid so. We went over this earlier. We cannot allow—"

The door flew open. "I am sick and tired of stupid rules like this. You people boss everyone around. I knew it was a mistake coming here. These places are all alike. I'm getting my son and leaving."

Her reaction stunned me.

"Wait, you don't have to go. You can smoke outside on our back deck like everyone else. We have chairs and shade trees."

"You can't make me do anything," she said, gathering her bags. "I'm getting my son and leaving."

I tried to reason with her, but she refused. I thought her back ached. She was tired. She needed a bed. Surely, a place to sleep and warm meals were worth a few rules. I didn't understand. Where would they stay so late in the day?

I walked outside and explained the situation to Danny. "Can you talk with your mother and convince her to stay until morning? It will be hard for you to find another shelter tonight. You won't have anywhere to go."

"Talking won't change anything," he said, kicking a rock. "When Mom gets upset, we move on. She won't listen to anybody. Besides, we sleep in our car. That's where we sleep most of the time, anyway."

"You don't go to school?"

He shook his head. "Nah, Mom teaches me. We have books in the car. She won't stay any place long enough for me to go to school. We only stop when her back hurts. Or when money runs out at the end of the month."

"You have income?"

"Mom gets disability, but it doesn't go very far. It pays our gas. We eat at soup kitchens a lot."

I was dumbfounded. Why would a mother want to raise her child in a station wagon? I pulled out a business card, giving it to Danny. "No matter where you are, call me if you get stranded or need help. I'll come and get you."

Danny stuffed the card in his pocket and glanced toward the lodge. His mother, fully energized now, burst out the front door and charged across the lawn with her many bags.

"Get in the car, Danny," she yelled. "We're leaving." He threw the ball to Josh and ran toward the car. A couple of minutes later, they were driving down the alley in their station wagon with Danny waving goodbye from the back window.

Josh came over to me. "Dad, I'm really sad for him. Danny told me he hates driving around all the time. He wants to live in a house and go to school like other kids. He wishes he had friends, but his mom won't stay anywhere long enough."

"I feel sad for him, too," I said, laying my hand on his shoulder. "I love you, son."

"I love you, too, Dad."

Josh went back to shooting baskets and I walked toward the lodge. Within seconds, a powerful accusation rose within me:

*You failed, and now Danny has to grow up in a station wagon. Why couldn't you convince Darlene to stay? What are you doing here? You're wasting your time. You don't have the ability to do this work. You barely understand it. You should get out before you hurt someone. Danny needs a home. And friends. But now he has nothing.*

Was it the great accuser? Or me? Overwhelmed, I couldn't focus. The questions pounded against me in waves.

At the desk, I couldn't get the accusations to stop. I finally gathered my papers and crammed them into my briefcase. I knew I had to leave. I needed to be alone for awhile. If I didn't win this battle, my work at the mission would soon be over. How could I sit back and watch people drag their children through a wasteland of stupidity? I felt my heart breaking over Danny and his lost dreams.

In the past few months we'd seen wonderful changes taking place in the lives of our residents. We talked about it at our staff meetings. Yet at that moment, nothing else mattered. The pain and loneliness in Danny's eyes—and the ominous fear I made things worse—overshadowed anything positive.

I felt like someone had kicked me in the stomach. I called Elaine to cover my shift.

When she arrived, I took Josh and we drove home.

# EIGHTEEN

## A Dung Heap

The look on Danny's face as he waved goodbye from the back of his station wagon was a picture I wouldn't soon forget. I dropped Josh off at home and drove to a nearby wooded area with hiking trails. Parking my car, I found a solitary path and started walking. It led me to a small bluff overlooking the Sangamon River.

Thankful to be alone, I found a flat place to sit above the flowing water below, and hung my feet over the edge. Now I could plead my case.

*Lord, I need you to answer the charges laid out against me. Are the accusations true? If you want me to continue in this work, I need your wisdom and strength to keep going.*

I watched the water swishing over the smooth rocks below.

"Danny is just a boy," I shouted across the river, "so much like Josh, with so much potential, except he's trapped. Things might be different now if I'd said the right things. But instead, I failed. Now all he has is a dung heap." I kicked my heels against the rock formation.

Amidst the rippling water, amidst the rustling trees, I heard a gentle whisper in my spirit.

*I'm the God of dung, too.*

You're the God of dung? I wondered.

*What you see as mere waste, I see as fertilizer. Out of fertilizer, the most beautiful things grow.*

Corn and beans? The fields of my childhood came to mind.

*Remember the lessons of your grandfather. Do you remember the day he took you down to the cattle lot, and you both shoveled cow droppings into his farm wagon? Remember the smell?*

How could I forget a smell like that? One of my rites of passage was helping Grandpa spread cow pies across the 200-acre field he sharecropped.

*Remember when you asked your grandfather, "Why are we doing this?" Instead of answering your question, he pulled his wagon onto the field and gave you two simple rules:"Don't look back and keep your mouth shut."*

Of course I remembered. Grandpa would throttle up the engine, lift his foot to release the clutch, then yank a rope and pull a lever. Off we went. The first time I saw that old manure spreader slinging cow pies in every direction, my mouth gaped open.

I only made *that* mistake once.

Wow, I hadn't thought about that in years. I loved riding with Grandpa. How could I not spend time with the man who breathed love into my life? Monday through Friday, he'd drive into town to pick up me and my three sisters for school. Later, he'd show up and drive us home. He wanted to be a part of our lives, hear how our day went.

I missed Grandpa's rough, chapped hands. Hands that helped guide me into manhood.

*Remember what your grandfather taught you about manure? Those same lessons apply to life in a fallen world.*

Grandpa knew a lot about manure.

*When your grandfather said, "Manure is necessary for growth," he was right. In the same way, the difficult situations in life—the manure—lead you to wisdom, maturity and completeness. They help you grow, causing you to lack nothing.*

Wow, I had never thought about manure like that before.

*The accuser lies to you, Scott. He says you are failing—at my job. It's not your responsibility to make people do the right thing. You cannot command or create a harvest. Your job is to create an environment where I can be seen, where my love is shown. I will take care of the rest.*

Hearing these words, tears spilled down my face. God had given me the answer I needed. Watching the ebb and flow of the water below, I heard his last words:

*Remember what your grandfather taught you: "We can prepare the fields for seeds. We can plant the seeds. We can even water the seeds. But we cannot make the seeds grow. That's in God's hands." Your grandfather was a wise man. He understood my truth.*

After a brief silence I climbed down and brushed myself off. A scripture passage came to mind about planting and harvest. Later, at home, I found it in 1 Corinthians, chapter 3. Reading it aloud, more tears flowed. I had never applied this simple truth before. Now it seemed alive and practical and relevant. I would read this scripture many times in the future. It would become part of my life, and shape my outlook on ministry.

> What, after all, is Apollos? And what is Paul, only servants through whom you came to believe—as the Lord has assigned to each his task. I planted the seed, Apollos watered it, but God has been making it grow. So neither the one who plants nor the one who waters is anything, but only God, who makes things grow. The one who plants and the one who waters have one purpose, and they will be rewarded according to their own labor. For

we are co-workers in God's service; you are God's field, God's building.[1]

These words set me free to continue in homeless ministry. That day, I received a clear understanding of *our* responsibility. Like farming, our work with the homeless demands faith. A letting go. We plant, we water, but only God can bring the increase.

Our job is to create an environment ideal for growth—a place where the love of God could be seen and felt, where his power can work freely.

We are called to be environmentalists.

The freedom I found in that simple truth made all the difference in ministry. We would have to redefine success. No longer could we measure it by a single outcome.

For too long, we believed success had to be a radical transformation. A life completely changed, set on a path of lasting joy and peace.

That's still our desire, of course, but in our job of planting and watering, we had to develop new markers for success. The truth is, we might not see the harvest. It might happen at a later date. Or someplace else. Or maybe not at all.

With this revelation I had to reexamine my motives. Was I helping people out of love from a pure heart? Or was I doing it out of selfish desires? Did I have to see the harvest with my own eyes to feel successful, to feel good about myself? Or could I plant and water, knowing others in the kingdom of God might reap the harvest?

I am so grateful for God's wisdom. A loving Father in heaven gave me exactly what I needed to become effective in homeless ministry.

When my world brushed up against Danny's for that brief instant, it changed the expectations I placed on myself and my staff. The next day, I walked into work with a brand new quest: We are environmentalists. That means we stop taking responsibility for other people's actions. We stop blaming ourselves when someone self-destructs.

Our job is to maintain an atmosphere of love at all times. And no matter the response, our love must continue to flow. *That's* our measure of success.

Connie and the staff embraced this concept with open arms. It would become the backdrop of our ministry to the homeless. With this new revelation, our prayers at the mission would change. Now we simply ask:

*Lord, allow the fruit of your Spirit to flow out of our lives, so people can see you. In Jesus' name.*

# NINETEEN

## Ashes for Life

Several weeks after Danny's sudden departure, I was working alone one afternoon in the lodge office. Earlier that day a group from a nearby church had taken our residents to our local swimming pool for an outing. I had already arranged for the lodge supervisor on duty and two staff members to accompany them.

The lodge, quieter than usual, gave me an opportunity to catch up on paperwork. Engrossed in my task, I didn't notice anyone coming up our front steps. A sudden pounding on the front door jolted me to my feet.

Opening the door, I stood face to face with a brawny, broad-shouldered woman sporting tattoos on her arms and a bandana around her head. A lanky man hovered behind her with two children. The woman, taking the lead, stepped forward.

"Got any rooms?" she asked, crossing her arms powerfully.

I couldn't help but notice the "Born to Raise Hell," tattoo running up her forearm. It looked homemade, like something created in a dark garage. The woman's black tee shirt, flaunting a skull-and-bones emblem, revealed biceps bigger than mine. The man behind her remained stooped in her shadow.

*Lord, are you sure about this?*

I welcomed them in. "Your timing is perfect," I said, wishing I felt grateful. "A room opened up yesterday. Are you married?"

"See for yourself," she said brusquely. The woman took out a raggy piece of paper from her back jeans pocket and shoved it in my face. "See here. Clarice and Edmond Russell. We're married."

"Great, I'll make a copy with your IDs when we fill out paperwork."

As grace dictates, we offer an empty room to the next person or family coming to our door. We had stopped taking names and holding spots for people years ago since most move on by the time we have an opening. Now, we simply trust God and his timing to fill our rooms.

"My name is Scott," I said, offering my hand to shake.

The woman clamped onto my fingers, making me wince. "Call me Clare, and this is my husband, Eddie. That's my daughter, Rose, and my son, Red."

Both had reddish hair and freckles and looked to be about the same age, seven or eight. Eddie, standing behind Clare, moved to the left where I could see him. His eyes stayed on the floor. I noticed a golf-ball-like swelling on his left jaw and a few tattoos on his arm, nothing as bold as Clare's.

"I hope your room is big enough for the four of us," Clare said, as if she had a room reserved at the Hilton.

"Well, the room isn't huge, but it has a set of bunk beds with a trundle underneath. I wish we could offer you more floor space, but none of our rooms are large. Come into the office and we can start the paperwork."

Clare didn't move and Eddie stayed in his place behind her. "I want to see the room before we sign anything," she said. "I don't know if we want to stay here yet."

Her brashness stunned me. The likelihood of this family doing well looked slim.

"No problem. Follow me. The room's in the basement." I took them through the kitchen to the back staircase and led them downstairs. With a tinge of guilt, I hoped they wouldn't like the room. I'd worked with people long enough to recognize defiance, and Clare already showed the signs.

I unlocked the room and stepped back. Clare marched in, going directly to the bunk beds. She pounded each twin mattress with her fist, and then pulled out the trundle bed. "Looks decent enough," she said, flipping the mattress. "Red and Rose can sleep at each end." She inspected the closet and the dresser, opening every door and drawer.

She straightened. "Where's the bathroom?"

"In the hallway." I pointed out the doorway. "We have a bath at both ends of the hall. Yours is right there." Eddie leaned over and mumbled something in Clare's ear.

"Okay, we'll stay," she said, moving toward the door. "Let's get the paperwork over with."

On our way to the office, I anticipated at least one uprising during the intake process. To my surprise, we completed everything without a problem. Afterward, Clare made a pronouncement: "We want nothing to do with a Christian organization. We're here only out of necessity."

With her eyes fastened on me, she stood. Eddie and the kids followed her lead.

"We don't trust religious people, especially Christians. We'll go to your Bible studies if we have to, but don't expect us to like 'em or agree with 'em."

"That's fine. Just keep in mind, the majority of our donors are Christian folks who care about this ministry. We ask our residents to show respect to those providing their housing."

She scowled. "Fair enough."

"Great. Welcome to the mission. I hope you'll like it here."

That afternoon the Russell family moved into the basement.

Soon after, we felt tension in the shelter. Clare carried a sort of restless chaos with her that was hard to contain. No matter where she went, it spilled onto others. We hoped to get to know the Russells better, but they wouldn't make it easy.

A few days after moving in, Clare came into the lodge office, going straight to her and Eddie's locker. Connie and I had worked the overnight shift, so we were both in the office with our two youngest boys finishing up breakfast. Our older kids had gone to the kitchen to eat with their friends.

Connie took this opportunity to engage Clare.

"So how are you this morning?"

"Fine, but Eddie needs his meds." Clare opened two prescription bottles, shaking out a pill from each. "He's in a foul mood and doesn't want to get out of bed."

"He's so quiet and gentle, that surprises me."

Connie tried to give Isaac his last bite of scrambled eggs, but he grabbed the spoon and stuffed it in his mouth. I chuckled to myself.

"Eddie doesn't talk around new people," Clare explained. "Once he gets to know you, he might say something. If he trusts you."

"Where did you and Eddie meet?"

"California. We're both from Illinois, but we met there. We left bad situations here. I bumped into Eddie at a Hell's Angels poker run one day, and I guess the rest is history." She slammed the locker door shut. "We had a lot in common. A weird bond, I guess." Her hoarse laugh echoed through the lodge.

I set my empty plate aside. "What brought you back to Illinois?"

Clare tromped to the doorway. I felt the desk vibrate with each step.

"I need to run these meds down to Eddie. I'll be back."

Connie collected our dishes and went to the kitchen. I took Jake and Ike to the small bathroom in the back and washed their hands. "Okay, boys, grab your toys and let's go back into the office."

Connie helped me situate them on the floor. She didn't realize Clare had followed her back in.

I motioned toward the couch. "Feel free to take a seat."

Clare heaved out a raspy cough. Although in her mid-thirties, years of smoking had already affected her. She dropped onto the couch with a thud. "Sorry, the stairs get to me sometimes."

Connie smiled at her.

"Clare, you have the clearest, bluest eyes I've ever seen."

Until then, all I had noticed was her bulky, tattooed arms. She wasn't a person most of us would care to meet in an alley.

"Thanks," Clare said, fluttering her eyelids in a mocking way.

"What brought you back to Illinois?" I asked, going back to my last question.

"Cost of living, I guess. Eddie and I hoped to make money and find happiness in California, but that was a bust."

"You couldn't find jobs?" Connie asked.

"Let's just say...we worked at some money-making deals that paid our bills for awhile...nothing that lasted."

Clare shooed a fly buzzing around her head.

Connie grabbed the flyswatter and stood watch. She turned toward Clare. "Did you and Eddie have your children in California?"

"No, I had my kids before I met Eddie, but he loved 'em from the start and always treated 'em like his own."

"So you took your kids with you to California?" I asked.

"No, I went to California myself as a teenager. I wanted to be a movie star. Instead, I got pregnant with Red and Rose. They're twins. When I first got there, I met a nice group of people who watched out for me. I lived in my car across from their Hell's Angels hangout. They took me in and I did errands for them. Odd jobs and stuff. That's when I got pregnant."

Spotting the fly, Connie took a step toward Clare. "Was Eddie in California then?" she asked.

"No, he came six years later. I'm older than Eddie. He ran away from a state home at seventeen and showed up at the poker run. We started talking and hit it off. Before long, we moved in together. We later went to the justice of the peace and got married.

"We thought we had it made," she said, with a scoff. "Then things fell apart."

Connie swatted the fly on the wall behind Clare, making her jump. "Whoa, warn me next time," she said, swinging a fist in the air.

"Sorry." Connie laid the swatter aside and joined our boys on the floor. Gathering stray toys, she asked, "So what happened next?"

"I don't know, we lost our jobs. Our housing."

Connie and I glanced at each other, wondering what Clare left out. People often skip over the most important details.

"The Hell's Angels scene was too much for Eddie, so we moved to a different town. After that, nothing panned out. We couldn't find steady work, and things got real bad. We had nobody helping us out. That's why we came back here. I thought my relatives might take us in for awhile. Wrong. They told us they couldn't afford extra mouths to feed. Like that's all we are. Mouths."

Her bitter laugh turned into another cough.

Clare hoisted herself off the couch. "Well, enough of my trip down memory lane. I need to check on Eddie and go for a smoke."

Throughout that month, more of their story came out, much like puzzle pieces without a border. With each passing week, new dramas would unfold. Clare's mother called one day warning us not to believe anything her daughter said. Then relatives started showing up in the alley behind the mission, screaming back and forth with Clare. They drove off whenever we came around.

We just watched and prayed for the Russell family, waiting for clarity.

Then one morning Eddie came into the office by himself. Surprised at seeing him alone, I wanted to see if he would converse with me.

"Hi, Eddie," I said, trying to sound casual. I kept my eyes on the computer screen as he walked past me to his locker. I didn't want to intimidate him.

He didn't respond.

I made another attempt. "Good morning."

I barely heard his, "Hi, Scott," with his face buried in the locker. He took out a medicine bottle, opening it.

"Eddie, do you mind if I ask you a question?"

He shook out a pill, and then reached for another bottle.

"I'm wondering about the growth on your jaw. We have doctors in Springfield who specialize in things like that."

Eddie put his meds back and closed the locker door.

"We've helped others with medical issues in the past. Last summer Connie took a lady to Peoria to get a glass eye made."

He shuffled toward the middle of the room, slowing to a stop. He waited for me to finish.

"The lady had lost her eye in a drive-by shooting. It's a miracle the bullet only grazed her eye. The eye company donated their services and fit her with a perfectly-matched, hand-painted eye. Afterward, she threw her eye patch in the garbage can and cried. It changed her life."

Eddie, staring at the floor, scraped his faded boot back and forth on our threadbare carpet. I hated pushing him, but several of us had concerns about his health. Maybe it was a tumor or something.

"If you're interested, we could arrange for a doctor to look at your jaw. Have you had it checked out before?"

He scraped his boot again.

"Eddie, have you seen a doctor?"

"No," he said, in a low moan.

"Would you like to get it removed?"

Eddie took a step toward the door. I knew this wasn't easy for him.

"I ain't wantin' it gone," he murmured, being patient with me.

"We would like to help you with this. Do you know what it is?"

He inhaled deeply, letting it out slowly. "I know what it is, and it's fine."

Eddie took another step, trying to close the discussion.

"If you're worried about money, we have people who can help you with this. It wouldn't be a problem."

He scuffed the carpet, taking one more step. I almost didn't hear his next words.

"It's all I got left of my family."

What did he say? I wanted to understand.

"The growth on your face is all you have left of your family? What do you mean?"

With two more scuffs, Eddie reached the doorway. I thought our conversation was over. Instead, he closed both halves of the double door and shuffled to the couch, sitting on the edge. He leaned forward, resting both elbows on his knees. His eyes found a spot on the floor between his feet.

I waited, wondering if he would speak. A minute later, his gravelly words fell into a slow, mechanical rhythm.

"When I was a boy, my dad had a' office in the back o' our house. I turned eleven that day and walked in without askin'. Dad got angry and yelled, 'Git out! Don't come in here 'less I *say* you can.' So I said my 'pologies and left."

Eddie rocked gently, remembering.

"Later, Ma told me fetch Dad for dinner. I forgot all about his warnin' and walked in without knockin'. I know it was stupid, but I'm glad I did."

"Why's that?"

"Dad laid eyes on me and reached for his pellet gun and shot me in the face. He cussed at me and hollered, 'Maybe next time you'll stay outta here when I'm workin'.' The pellet hit me right here in my jaw." Eddie rubbed his jaw, grimacing. "Felt like fire.

"When Dad saw he shot my face, he called me over and checked me out. He said, 'Git a band-aid on it and shut up. You ain't wantin' anybody takin' ya from us, do ya?'

"So that's what I did. I tol' Ma I jabbed myself with a stick outside playin', and she believed me. That was twenty-one years ago. I still have the pellet in my jaw. It's gittin' bigger, but I ain't wantin' it out."

"Why would you care about anyone finding out now? It's not a threat anymore."

Eddie rocked harder. "Three days after Dad shot me, I walked home from school and seen black smoke hangin' over my neighborhood. I ran fast as I could to see where it come from.

"When I reached my neighbor's yard, I stopped cold. I couldn't move 'cause o' what I saw."

He rocked fiercely now.

"Men carryin' black bags outta my front door. They laid 'em 'cross my yard. I knew what they were. I watched 'nough TV to know a body bag when I seen one.

"My house was charcoal. Burnt like toast. And my family dead. I don't 'member nothin' else that day. Neighbors said I ran 'round crazy, yellin' for my brothers. Someone said a po-leeceman shoved me in a car and drove me to the hospital. All I 'member, Granddad came and got me later."

I listened to Eddie, flabbergasted.

"Dad had a meth lab in our house. He used his office for soo-pplies and sales. Po-leece said he had a slip-up cookin' the meth. Dad caused the 'splosion that killed my family.

"I'm alive today 'cause I stayed after school for dee-tention." Eddie looked away, stoic. I could see the pain in his muscles, flexing and twitching, making him want to run again.

"Granddad yelled and cried. I never saw 'im act like that before. He scared me. He told me how sorry he was, but couldn't raise me. He sent me to Mawn-tana to live with rel'tives I ain't never seen before. Granddad said I should leave my memories 'hind and start over."

Eddie stopped rocking and eased himself off the couch. For the first time, his eyes locked into mine.

"I don't think my life ever started up 'gain after that." He turned toward the door.

My mind listened, but I couldn't comprehend. My world, so safe and sheltered, collided with a world beyond my understanding.

Eddie rested against the doorframe long enough to say, "I told ya more 'n I cared to, but now ya know. Please don't ask again."

Then he disappeared.

# TWENTY

## The Eruption

The Russell family stayed at the mission for five months. Neither Clare nor Eddie opened up again after their initial conversations with us. Much about their lives remained a mystery. Yet, we all sensed Clare's anger under the surface. For some reason, she carried a special disdain for Christians. We tried to help, but nothing seemed to calm her simmering rage.

The day Clare decided to move her family out, I became the target of her fury. I walked in the front door that morning and saw the Russells carrying boxes out the back. Since I had no prior warning, I wanted to find out what prompted their sudden move.

"They sold some of their belongings over the week-end," Elaine explained from the desk. "They put a deposit down on an apartment. That's all they would tell me."

I shook my head. "I don't know how they can last out there. Clare works thirty hours a week at minimum wage and Eddie can't find steady work."

"I wish I knew more," she said, collecting her stuff. "Clare refused to fill out an exit form. I gave her my phone number and told her to call if she needs anything, but I'll be surprised if I hear from her."

Elaine turned her head, calling out, "Kimi, we need to go."

Her daughter emerged from the back room carrying her book bag.

"I didn't know you were here," I said, giving Kimi a pat on the shoulder. She grinned.

"We need to run," Elaine said. "I have to drive Kimi to school. The lodge is yours, Scott. See you in a couple of days."

"Have a good week, ladies." I seated myself behind the desk and opened my briefcase. Hearing a noise, I looked up and saw Clare walking toward me. She laid her room key on the desk.

"All we have left is our medicine," she said, opening their locker. She dumped its contents into a brown paper bag.

"So where are you moving?"

"That's none of your business." She slammed the locker door shut. "We're done here."

"Okay, but if things get tough out there—"

"We'll be fine," Clare interrupted. "We have our own place now. We don't need your charity." She took a few steps toward the door, then stopped halfway and spun around.

"If you want the truth, Scott—and I know you like the truth—we can't stand being here anymore. We're sick of your Bible studies, the smiling and the laughing, and all the fake stuff you guys do. Nobody's real around here, especially you. You think you're Mr. High and Mighty Christian, and this place is your castle. The rest of us are peons."

I underestimated Clare's disdain. With each word, her voice escalated.

"Honestly, you can cram all your holier-than-thou…."

Without a blink, she unleashed a fury of expletives in combinations I hadn't heard before. Her rage, built up for who-knows-how-long, spewed such rapid-fire venom, it actually impressed me. I sat at the desk, amazed. I didn't know anyone capable of slinging so many disgusting words and foul statements in one breath.

Listening, I realized how marvelous God's timing is. He had prepared me for a moment like this. Had it happened earlier, before Danny and the lessons there, her accusations might have crushed me. The sheer force of her fury would have melted me under the weight of my messianic complex.

Yet now, in the midst of her outburst, I knew we did everything possible to help Clare's family. We created an atmosphere of love using the limited information they gave us to offer practical help and hope for a new life.

We were, and still are, environmentalists. Our role of planting and watering allows people like Clare to either accept or reject what we offer. It's not personal. That knowledge allowed me to pray for Clare, even as I sat listening to her rant.

*Lord, how can I plant more seed into Clare's life before she leaves?*

A Bible verse from Matthew came to mind, one I'd heard many times. I smiled as I remembered these words of Jesus:

> Blessed are you when you are persecuted for righteousness sake, for yours is the kingdom of heaven. Blessed are you when they revile and persecute you, and say all kinds of evil against you falsely for my sake. Rejoice and be exceedingly glad. For great is your reward in heaven, for so they persecuted the prophets who were before you.[1]

"What are you smiling about?" Clare shouted. "Can't you hear me?"

"Yes, I can, and thank you for blessing me."

Her jaw clenched. She glared at me.

"Jesus says I'm blessed when you say all kinds of evil against me. He says to rejoice and be glad. So thank you for blessing me."

I couldn't stop smiling.

The look on Clare's face prepared me for round two. I jumped in first.

"We didn't make you homeless, Clare, and your rage isn't about me or the mission. It's about *you* and *your* life. But you aren't willing to face that truth about yourself."

Her face turned fiery red, but I finished.

"If you want to blame me for your problems, go ahead. I just hope and pray you get tired of your rage and lay it down someday. I pray God blesses you and your family. I wish you the best."

Clare fired another round of curses, identifying me as anything but a man. She followed with words about my mother, my family, and my belief system—telling me what I could do with myself and the mission—which I'm sure are physically impossible.

To this day I measure every caustic attack and cussing against the one I received from Clare. Most can't compare in creative ability.

Wheezing and hollering her way out of the building, Clare's voice faded down the alley to where her family waited in a taxi.

Silence fell upon the lodge.

All of us inside watched the Russell family drive away. Three of our resident ladies, witnessing the verbal attack, came over to comfort me.

"Mr. Scott, are you okay?" they asked, patting me.

"I really am, thank you. I feel sad for the Russells because they refuse to see the truth of their circumstances. But I believe we did our job. We used the gifts God gave us to create the best possible environment. The rest is out of our hands."

The ladies agreed.

"This is the only place I ever felt loved and accepted," a mom in her thirties said. "I love it here."

"Me, too," an older woman said. "This is what home is supposed to feel like."

"I'm glad you feel that way, because we're all family here. And every one of you is an important part. The Russell family chose to leave, and that's okay. We cannot force Clare, or any of you for that matter, to stay and respond the way we want. It's your choice."

They hugged me.

"The only thing we can do now is pray for the Russells. We cannot assume God is finished with them yet."

# TWENTY-ONE

## Surprise Visitor

Clare's brazen exit revealed a rage we hadn't seen before in a resident. She made Elaine's revolt against curfew look docile. After Clare left, Connie and I assumed we'd never see her again.

Yet we discovered a valuable truth. Some people must return to their old ways of living before they're willing to change. They arrive at the mission, stay for awhile, and see their lives beginning to improve. The crisis is over and everything's under control. It's time to move on. They no longer want or need our help. Except this time when they go out, their darkness looks darker. They'd been exposed to the light of God's love.

The contrast can be overwhelming.

When speaking to churches now, I often say, "Living back on the street is sometimes the best softening agent God uses to bring people to him." And then I explain.

We learned this truth about ten months after the Russells' departure. Connie and I sat in worship one Sunday at South Side Christian Church singing the opening song. Before the second stanza, Connie elbowed me and nodded toward the other side of the auditorium. I couldn't believe what I saw: Clare sitting in a pew with a lady from our Sunday school class. She was the last person I expected to see in church, especially *our* church.

*Lord, what's going on?*

When she left the mission, she hated Christians. Why did Clare now sit in a place she claimed to loathe? She had refused our offer of church, saying it gave her the creeps. What changed? My gaze caught her attention, and she appeared to cringe. Connie and I waved at her. She averted her eyes, staring at the lyrics on the big screen.

"Maybe I can talk to her after the service," I whispered. "She may try to duck out, so I'll head over after the closing song."

"Okay, I'll get the kids."

I tried to concentrate on the sermon, but my mind kept drifting back to Clare. No matter why she came, I wanted to welcome her and let her know we didn't hold a grudge.

When the last song ended, I hurried across the auditorium and found her halfway down the aisle talking with another lady from our Sunday school class. I waited until they finished, then stepped up beside her.

"Hi, Clare. It's great to see you. How did you like the service?"

"Good. As usual. I like it here."

"Really? I haven't seen you here before."

She shrugged. "This isn't my first time."

My eyes probed hers, wanting more.

"Okay, I'll tell you," she said. "I saw you and Connie here a couple of weeks ago. That scared me, so after the service, I high-tailed it outta here and almost didn't come back."

"Why?"

"Because of the things I said to you when I left." Her cheeks turned red. "I figured you'd tell everyone here at the church and run me out."

I laughed. "That's not my style. As far as I'm concerned, that's water under the bridge. No hard feelings."

"Really?" she said, brightening. "I'm glad, because I like this place. A lady invited me to Sunday school my first week here, and

I met some really nice people in the Friendship Class. That's why I came back."

"The Friendship Class?" I said, incredulous. "That's *our* Sunday school class."

"Mine, too, now."

Connie and I attended the Friendship Class whenever our schedule allowed. We would often present the work of the mission at other churches, or we'd fill in for other Sunday school teachers, so we weren't always in class. We had no idea she was attending.

"That's great," I said, trying not to show surprise. "How did you end up here at South Side? We have tons of churches in the area."

"Well, that's a long story. I'd tell you, but Eddie and the kids are in the truck waiting on me, and they're hungry." She turned toward the exit, walking away.

"How about next week? Connie and I will be in class."

"I'll be here," she said, over her shoulder.

Later, driving home, I told Connie, "Clare seems to have a different attitude. I don't know what happened, but she plans to explain next week. Maybe we can get here early."

She laughed. "We can certainly try."

The following Sunday, we dropped Jacob and Isaac off at their preschool rooms, and headed toward the Friendship Class. Our older children had already gone to their own classes.

Tony, our teacher, greeted us with a friendly handshake. "Good morning, Paynes. It's great to have you back."

"Thanks, Tony. We'll be here next week, too," I said, "but I can't promise anything. This morning, we lost a shoe and had to search for two Bibles. I'm always surprised when we make it anywhere on time, let alone early." He laughed.

We strolled over to the coffee counter and spotted Clare sitting at a back table. Connie left to go join her. Clare already had a cup of coffee and a doughnut in front of her.

Filling two Styrofoam cups, I carried our coffee to the table, greeting class members on my way. I took a seat next to Connie, sliding her cup over.

"Hi, Scott," Clare said, taking a bite of her doughnut.

"Hey, it's great to see you again. I have to admit, you surprised me last Sunday."

"Well, no one's more surprised than me."

"Why is that?"

Clare glanced down at her tattoos and neon shirt featuring a rock band I didn't recognize.

"I never thought a church would accept me."

Her eyes welled up, which amazed me. She never let us see this side of her at the mission.

"South Side is a good place for you. It's a family-oriented church, and if you let them, they'll welcome you in."

"I'm sorry for all those things I said to you before I left. I hated the world. I hated *my* world. And I took it out on you and the mission."

"People change and grow, Clare. I forgive you and I'm sure Connie does, too."

"I do," Connie said, with a cheerful nod.

"So what brought you to South Side?" I asked.

Clare looked at the clock. "I'd better talk fast."

We huddled closer. The noise level had increased with more people arriving.

"Four weeks ago today, I drove across town to visit my mom. I'm still trying to connect with family—a real hoot—but I won't go into that now. I was driving our old pickup truck that morning and turned onto MacArthur Boulevard going south. Well, I didn't get too far down the road before it sputtered a few times and lost power, which shocked me. The truck had never done that before.

"I coasted as far as I could and finally parked it right here beside the church.

"My first thought was, of all the places to break down, why did it have to be a church? I got out and raised the hood to check the engine. I fiddled with it for awhile, but that thing was dead. I wanted to scream. When I got back in the truck, I pounded on the steering wheel and said a few words I won't repeat here."

She looked sheepish. "You've heard them."

I suppressed a smile.

"At least the truck was off the main road and out of traffic," Connie said.

"Yeah, but at that moment I was furious at life. I have to admit, after leaving the mission, things got worse. We barely made enough money to pay rent, let alone feed the kids. I had to stand in line at those freebie places every week just to survive. I did that in California, too, but for some reason it felt pathetic here. No one seemed to care or understand. I felt so alone in life.

"On top of that, our rent was two months late and the kids needed shoes for school. I had no money and no one to call but Eddie. I knew my relatives wouldn't come. What I really needed was a phone, but I didn't see a person in sight. Only the church building.

"And then I realized I wore my black leather vest showing all my tatts. I could've kicked myself. What would people in the church say if I walked in?"

Clare looked at Connie.

"If you didn't know me, what would you think if I came into church like that? Well, don't answer."

Her husky laugh filled the room.

Connie almost choked on her coffee. "You know I liked you from the beginning."

"That's why I asked you instead of Scott."

She snorted, clapping her hand over her mouth. "Sorry."

We laughed again.

"Anyway, I didn't want to take the risk or scare anyone," Clare said, "but then I thought, wait, churches are supposed to help people. Maybe they'd let me use a phone.

"So I braced myself for the worst and left the truck. I walked around to the back of the church, hoping to sneak in, but when I reached the door, it opened. A woman greeted me with a huge smile, saying, 'Welcome to South Side.' She shook my hand and pulled me into the building like I was her long, lost friend. I couldn't believe she didn't notice how I looked.

"She said her name was Annie, and I saw something flash in her mouth. A tongue-ring, I think, which shocked me. If a church can accept *her*, maybe they'd let me use a phone.

"I must've looked uptight since Annie asked if I was okay. I explained my situation, and told her, 'I just want to use a phone and get out of the building before anyone sees me.'

"Annie laughed and grabbed my arm, saying, 'We have a phone you can use, but I'm not letting you call anyone until you go to Sunday school class with me. It's just down the hall.' She practically dragged me to this room. After walking in, I felt like I had to stay."

"I'm picturing you being dragged down the hall," Connie said, with a grin.

"Well, you can bet I protested all the way. I kept saying, 'I'm not dressed right. These people are different from me.' Annie just laughed and said, 'Do I look like a fashion goddess? You're clothed. That's all that matters.'

"She was right. When I walked in, everyone welcomed me. Two ladies even hugged me. I didn't know a church could be that friendly.

"After class, Annie let me call Eddie, but he couldn't get here for an hour. She asked me if I'd sit with her in the worship service, and I did. I really like it.

"The funny thing is when Eddie got here, the truck started right up. He couldn't find anything wrong with it. The engine still runs great."

I felt sure God had guided Clare here. Annie was the perfect person for her to meet. She loved people and knew how it felt to be at the mercy of others. She had stayed at the mission herself during a rough season in her life.

"Looks like you're meant to be here," Connie said. "I think you're good for the people here, too."

"They have no idea what they're getting." Clare said, with a raspy laugh. "It shocked me how much the Friendship Class made me feel welcome. They even invited me back. This is my fourth week now."

The class quieted as Tony opened his Bible at the small podium.

"Maybe Eddie and your kids will come here, too," Connie whispered.

Clare frowned. "I don't know about that."

"Can you stay after class?" I asked. "I have one more question."

She agreed, and we turned our attention to Tony.

During his lesson, I thought about Clare. Her attitude changed after leaving the mission. What made the difference? Was it the warm, friendly atmosphere she found here in the Friendship Class? If so, God works in mysterious ways. We had offered a warm, loving environment at the mission, yet she rejected it.

What did she leave out of her story? No matter what, Clare seemed less angry now.

*Thank you, Lord, for bringing Clare here. Help her find freedom from her past. In Jesus' name.*

# TWENTY-TWO

## An Emerging Thread

After the closing prayer, class members gathered their belongings and made their way to the auditorium. Connie, Clare, and I stayed to finish our conversation.

I refilled our coffee cups and moved to the chair across from Clare. "Okay, I'm curious. Why did you leave the mission last year in such a fury?"

She leaned back in her chair.

In a quiet, reflective voice, she said, "You guys are different from me. When I first met you, I couldn't handle it. You had so much, it hurt knowing I could never have that. Inside, I felt this rage I never felt before, and it kept building. The longer we stayed, the worse it got.

"That's why I exploded when we left."

"I guess our old van looks pretty good to someone who has nothing," I said, thinking I understood.

She scowled. "It's not your stuff, Scott. It's your family. You have people who love you and want to be around you. People you love back. Don't you realize how hard it is for someone like me, who's never had a real family, to watch people like you?"

Clare's clear blue eyes, glossy with tears, pierced through mine.

"My family broke apart and scattered before I was old enough to know what happened. I can't remember half the people who raised me. There were seven of us kids, and we were split up and moved around so much, I have no idea where most of us lived.

"We stayed with Mom some, but we got farmed out to shirt-tail relatives or foster homes whenever her addictions flared up. Mom was a pill addict, so you can figure the math. That was our life."

"What about your father?" Connie asked.

"My dad took off when I was real young. I doubt if I could recognize him in a police line-up. All I remember is him leaving and Mom starting in with the pills. I hated her drugged-out comas and her good-for-nothing men. My only prayer as a child was for a nice family that would love me and want me. But I never got that. I thought it was *my* fault. God couldn't give me something I didn't deserve."

Her tears rolled down, and Connie slid a napkin toward her.

"When I saw your family, it made me furious. Every day at the mission, I saw how you guys loved each other, how you got along, and how you laughed together. My anger boiled to the point I couldn't take it anymore. I had to get away from the mission before I hurt somebody.

"Even worse, you were Christian. I couldn't trust you. I lived with a Christian family once, and it was like being in a prison camp. Nothing I did was right. I had to endure all their weird punishments for hours on end.

"I remember having to sit in a bathtub full of ice water for hours after church on Sundays because I talked during the sermon or wouldn't go up and sing in front of people. They also made me stand on a two-by-eight in their blazing hot attic for hours. It was only two inches wide and they told me I'd fall through the insulation if my foot slipped. It scared me to death. I thought I could die any moment.

"After that, I wanted nothing more to do with churches or Christians."

She pressed the napkin against her face.

"When I met you guys, it confused me. I really longed for what you have, but I didn't want to believe nice Christians existed in this world. That's why on the day we left, I tried to burn every bridge I could on my way out. I had to face my reality and accept it. How could I even hope for a loving family like yours? I had to close that door before you slammed it in my face."

With a coarse laugh, she added, "But I guess God has different plans for me, huh?"

Connie reached over, patting her.

"Coming here made me face the truth. Nice Christians *do* exist, and they really *do* care about me. Deep down, I want good people in my life, but it still scares me.

"Last week, when you forgave me, Scott, you made me believe it wasn't too late. Even though I'm in my thirties, maybe I can still have people in my life who care about me, who won't hurt me."

Her eyes went to the floor.

"I'm sorry for the cussing I gave you. I don't know why I'm so stupid sometimes."

"Look at me, Clare," I said. "Please hear what I'm saying. You aren't the same person you were ten months ago. You have a softness now that wasn't there before. Your Father in heaven is drawing you to him. He has so much more in store for you. The cussing you gave me is history. I forgave you long ago."

Getting up, I walked around the table to give Clare a hug. I felt her hot tears against my cheek. "Someday, I hope you can forgive all the people in your life who've hurt you."

Nodding, she wiped her tears.

On my way back to my chair, I grinned at her. "You still hold the record for the best cussing I ever received."

Clare's mouth dropped open, and we all roared with laughter.

"It shocked Eddie when I told him I cussed you out. He knows I usually save that for my relatives."

She cackled, making us laugh again.

"What about Eddie and your children?" Connie asked. "You said you wanted a family. Aren't they your family now?"

"Don't get me wrong, I love them with all my heart—and they love me—but Eddie has his own issues to deal with. He went through some horrific stuff as a boy. Stuff he won't talk about with anyone, not even me.

"Then later, after his parents and brothers died in the fire, he got into trouble and landed in a boys' detention center. He lived there for years and *nobody* cared about him.

"Really, we're just trying to figure out what family means. Most days, we're just struggling to survive."

Connie put an arm around her. "I hope you realize you're part of our family, now."

Her eyes welled again. "Yeah, I'm starting to get that. You guys shocked me when we stayed at the mission. No matter how I acted, you still cared about me and my family. No one had ever treated us like that before. I couldn't get it out of my head after we left."

Clare pointed at her cheeks. "These are happy tears now."

Noticing the time, we all stood to leave.

"Thank you for sharing your life with us," I said. "I know this wasn't easy, but you've helped us understand your world so much better."

"You're welcome, but I don't know why I told you all this. I must feel safe with you." She looked around the room. "Being here makes me feel safe, too."

We walked to the sanctuary together. Clare met up with Annie, sitting with her.

During the worship service, I found it hard to focus. The conversation with Clare kept replaying in my mind. Her rage about our family made me wonder about the other stories of the mission: Elaine's drug addiction, Heidi's abandonment, Danny's nomadic life, Eddie's traumas, and some of the others we'd worked with.

Thinking about each one, comparing them side by side, I realized for the first time, they had a common denominator. A thread that seemed to connect them.

I felt a tinge of excitement.

*Lord, are you opening my eyes?*

For the past three years, Connie and I had sought to understand homelessness. We had both recognized the issues ran deep—deeper than anything physical—yet we couldn't pinpoint the cause.

Now, it was becoming clear.

I wanted to talk with Connie and process this together. I needed her input.

Yet it would have to wait.

The service ended and two people came over to discuss a mission project. I stayed behind, answering their questions. Connie had left to pick up the children.

When our discussion ended, I headed toward the preschool department. On my way there I saw Rachel and Josh, our two oldest, standing in the hallway with several high school and junior high friends. "Don't go anywhere," I said, walking by them. "We're leaving soon."

Jacob and Isaac, seeing me coming down the hall, bolted ahead of Connie. "Whoa, boys, slow down." I took their hands. "Let's walk."

Connie smiled, glad to have my help. Six children are a wonderful blessing, but a lot of work even on easy days.

"Where are Caleb and Sarah?" I asked her.

"I think they're in the gym playing ball."

I gave the boys to Connie and walked into the gym. Sure enough, they were both running with basketballs, red-faced, and out of breath.

"Okay, kids, let's go." I scooped up a stray ball. "Put the basketballs away."

Later, piling into our van, the kids started talking about their morning. Our middle two, Caleb and Sarah, described children's church and how goofy the teachers were that day.

"They dressed up like David and Goliath," Sarah exclaimed from the back of the van.

"You should've seen it, Dad," Caleb said, laughing. "One of the stones flew out of the slingshot and bounced off a kid's forehead."

In my rear-view mirror, I saw his arm re-enacting the big hit.

Sarah giggled. "The rock was a marshmallow. I grabbed it and ate it."

Connie started to scold, but Caleb jumped in.

"Mom, all the kids ate marshmallows. They shot them out everywhere."

We laughed, picturing the scene.

Next, Jacob and Isaac talked about Miss Peggy's class, the class every child at South Side wanted to stay in. Jacob had graduated six months earlier at the age of four, but he still felt the loss. Before leaving, he gave Miss Peggy his favorite toy, a match-car nestled in a tiny gift box.

Making things worse, Isaac had recently moved into her class at age two.

"I thought you liked your new teacher," Connie said, looking back at Jacob.

"I do," he said, in a forlorn voice. "Miss Peggy gives better hugs. I miss story time."

"I love Miss Peggy!" Isaac shouted from his car seat.

"You can always go back for more hugs," Connie said. "She has plenty to spare."

"Okay," Jacob said, a bit happier.

Connie looked toward the back. "How were your classes?"

"We didn't have slingshots and marshmallows," Josh said, with a laugh.

"The junior high came into our high school class today," Rachel said. "A guy was talking about the camp. Josh isn't as excited about going as I am."

"That's okay," Connie said. "It's not for everybody. Your dad only went once or twice as a kid, but I loved it. I went every year. I even worked at camp for a summer."

"I want to go again," Caleb said.

Sarah chimed in. "Me, too."

My mind went back to the common thread in homelessness.

"All right, kids, it's my turn now. I need to talk to your mom for a minute."

I glanced over at Connie.

"For the past three years, we've asked God to help us understand the root cause of homelessness. I believe he just answered our prayers."

Her eyes widened. "Really?"

"Thanks to Clare, homelessness just came into focus."

We turned into the driveway.

"I suppose it has to wait."

"Yeah, let's talk after lunch when the boys go to sleep. This might take awhile."

# TWENTY-THREE

## The Mystery Unfolds

I washed lunch dishes while Connie laid our two youngest boys down for their naps. Afterward, we met in the living room where I greeted her with a glass of iced tea.

"You're so good to me," she said, sitting in her favorite rocking chair. "We should have plenty of time to talk. The girls left on a bike ride, and the boys are outside shooting baskets."

"Great." I took a seat on the couch, placing my tea next to hers on the small table between us.

"Let's see, where should I start?"

I relaxed for a moment, gathering my thoughts.

"Okay, earlier today, when Clare talked about her desire for a family and the anger she felt about ours, I couldn't get it out of my mind. I saw the faces of Danny, Heidi, and the many others we had worked with at the mission, and I started thinking about their stories.

"For the first time, I noticed they all had something in common. A thread that seemed to connect them."

I paused, hoping my epiphany wouldn't sound anticlimactic after all our discussions on homelessness.

Taking a deep breath, I announced, "They *all* lack a home."

I smiled at her, triumphant.

Connie halted her rocking to study my face. "Okay, um... great. Now, tell me something I don't know."

I chuckled at my absurdly obvious statement.

"Let me ask you a question," I said, changing gears. "What comes to mind when you hear the word, 'home?'"

She scanned the room. "Love. Family. Refuge. A place where I'm accepted and encouraged."

"Okay, what do you think about when you hear the word, 'house?'"

"I think about the structure we live in. The physical building."

"Good."

"Will the questions get harder?" she asked, with a twinkle in her eyes.

I laughed, moving on.

"Can you have a 'home' without a house?"

Connie picked up her tea, taking a sip.

"Well, when I go to visit my parents, I go to see *them*, not their house. They've lived in three different houses since I went to college, and I always feel at home no matter what house they live in."

"So there's a difference," I said.

"Yes. I think Clare verbalized it best this morning when she expressed her desire for a family like ours. She wasn't talking about our house or our stuff. She wants positive people in her life who love her and want the best for her, people she can count on."

Setting her tea down, Connie smiled. "I see where this is going. Clare wants a *home.*"

"Yes," I said, with an energetic nod, "and the irony about homelessness, is that every person coming to our door had *housing* at one time or another. They all had roofs over their heads, but few had homes."

She sat back, rocking lightly.

"That's actually kind of profound. I've never thought about it *causing* homelessness before. Yet how many people have we worked with, like Clare and Eddie, who grew up in houses devoid of love and kindness? Their horrific memories keep them struggling for years."

"More than I can name," I said, noticing something between the couch cushions. I dug out a quarter, two pennies, and an ace of spades.

Connie laughed.

"Now, on the flip side, do you remember when lightning struck the Clarks' house last year?"

"How could I forget?" she said. "You came home after a meeting saying Rob and Kathy were knocked out of bed the night before. You said their house had caught on fire."

"Yeah, it's a good thing they were volunteer fire fighters. They knew exactly what to do."

"Didn't they have smoke and water damage, too?"

"They did, and their house wasn't safe to live in. The Clarks had to find a place to stay until repairs could be made. People joked about them being homeless, but that really wasn't the case."

"I remember you saying they had plenty of family and friends helping them out. Didn't people argue over who would get to host them?"

"That's just it. Their house was damaged, but not their home. Their positive relationships were still intact. They had a whole network of caring people around them. And they both had jobs and a savings account. The Clarks weren't homeless. They were houseless for a time."

Connie reflected for a moment. "That makes me think of Mary and Joseph. They weren't homeless either."

"What do you mean?"

"Every Christmas, we hear someone say Jesus was homeless

because he had to be born in a stable. But that's not the case. Joseph and Mary were traveling to Bethlehem for the census where they had to register. They weren't destitute—Joseph worked a trade as a carpenter. They just needed a place to stay.

"They had to flee to Egypt after baby Jesus was born, but when God told them it was safe, they returned to Joseph's hometown of Nazareth. Like the Clarks, they were houseless for a time, but never really homeless. If anything, they carried their home with them."

"For some reason," I said, "people try to elevate homelessness to a level of nobility. They don't want to accept its broken reality."

"Well, if people could see what we see on a daily basis, they would change their minds. It's all about brokenness. I'm excited about your revelation. I can see how homelessness is a complete meltdown of family."

I reached for my tea. "It affects everything for them. Just look at the toxic surroundings they come out of: roaches, rats, gunshots in the night...street fights."

"What about the mold and lead paint in some of those old apartment buildings? And the food they eat? It's a wonder they survive at all."

"Then there's the arguing and strife on a daily basis," I said. "Between the addictions and the abuse, they never relaxed as kids. They grew up in a constant state of fear, never trusting anyone."

Connie shook her head. "I can't imagine living in that every day of my life. How traumatizing. It's sad to think most of our residents came out of that kind of environment."

"Yeah, it's total environmental dysfunction, and the kids carry it with them into adulthood. It becomes a cycle."

She stopped rocking.

"What about Elaine? Didn't she grow up in a nice neighborhood? I know her father wasn't around much, but she had a mother, a brother, and grandparents who loved her. She didn't live in a toxic environment."

"Yes, but once again, we see how the definition of God's love is so important. Instead of giving Elaine what she really *needed* for lasting joy and peace, her parents gave her tons of money, material possessions, and unlimited freedom."

"They had good intentions, don't you think?" Connie asked. "They tried to make up for her father's absence."

"Maybe so, but it didn't work." I put my empty glass down. "You can't solve a relational issue with material goods."

She nodded slowly "That makes sense. Elaine's life proves it. Material goods without boundaries set the stage for her to catapult into a life of pleasure and excess."

"Which came crashing down after her parents died," I said. "The inheritance money fueled her destructive lifestyle longer, but when it ran out, she had no one left who was willing to help her pick up the pieces."

"So really, Elaine caused her own homelessness, wouldn't you say? We've seen people come out of worse circumstances than hers and never become homeless."

"That's because she didn't appreciate the blessings she *did* have. Elaine spent most of her life demanding *more*—while partying non-stop—which eventually led to her downfall. I believe her homelessness was self-induced. Elaine used her father's absence as an excuse to be selfish, allowing her to justify her behavior for years. Rules and authority became her biggest enemy. That's why she stomped out of the mission when she first came."

"She certainly hated our curfew," Connie said, with a chuckle.

"Yeah, it took standing outside on our sidewalk all alone, before Elaine could see her path of destruction."

"Well, I'm just glad she took responsibility before it was too late. She's such a great person. Thinking about this now, I would say her rebellion played a bigger role in her homelessness than her addictions."

"I'm sure it did," I said. "Rebellion *was* her biggest addiction. Would you like more tea?"

"No, I'm fine, thanks."

In the kitchen I refilled my glass, thinking about the contrast between houselessness and homelessness. I stepped outside to check on the boys, still shooting baskets in the driveway. "Hi, Dad," Josh yelled, going for a shot.

"Watch me, Dad," Caleb shouted, trying to swipe the ball from his older brother. He missed and toppled to the ground, sprawling across the grass. The three of us laughed, and I went back inside.

"The boys are having fun," I told Connie in the living room. I set my tea down and grabbed the footstool.

"They always seem to find something fun to do."

I put my feet up, sitting back against the couch. "You know, organizations like the American Red Cross do a wonderful job helping the *house*less after major emergencies or natural disasters. At the mission we help the *home*less—people coming out of a traumatic, toxic environment, or those rejecting their families and self-destructing like Elaine. There's a big difference."

"I'm glad we're seeing this now," Connie said. "Homelessness is about a relational deficit, the lack of a home, not a physical calamity."

We heard scuffling outside our front window, and a basketball flew by. I stood and waved at the boys to move away from the house.

Connie stayed focused. "Okay, we've identified the two main types of homelessness we work with at the mission: *traumatic* homelessness and *self-induced* homelessness. What about *chronic* homelessness? They often end up on the street."

"Well, the chronic homeless can't seem to stabilize anywhere, even in shelters due to their mental issues and addictions. They tend to isolate themselves from society. Which reminds me, did I tell you about the lady I met at the Mayor's Task Force on Homelessness last week?"

"I don't think so."

"Thirty people came to this meeting: social service workers, concerned citizens, and a few homeless folks. We all came together to talk about the needs of the homeless in Springfield.

"The meeting started and the chairwoman introduced a homeless lady named Pat, giving her the floor.

Pat stood up and said, 'All I need is an address, a shower, and clean clothing. Then I can get a job and save money for my own place.'

She looked at us, waiting for a response.

"Several people nodded their approval, which prompted her to add, 'Springfield's a wealthy city with the state capitol. You should all be ashamed of yourselves that people like me don't have an address. I bet all of *you* live in big houses with plenty of space. All *I* need is something small where I can get my mail, make calls for work, and sleep.'

"Then she sat down.

"I thought her needs sounded simple enough, especially since we had a room open up at the mission. Taking the floor, I introduced myself as the executive director of Inner City Mission, a homeless shelter for single women, children, and their parents.

"'I have good news,' I said, turning toward Pat. 'We had a room open up today. I can drive you to the mission right after this meeting.'

"Pat's eyes got huge, and she said, 'Oh, I can't come today. I have to pack my things.'

"'That's okay,' I told her, 'you can move in tomorrow.'

"She shook her head and said, 'I can't go to a shelter. I need my privacy. I don't like sleeping next to people I don't know.'

"I explained, 'You won't be sleeping in a big room with other people. We have private rooms where you can have your own bed, a dresser, and a closet.'

"Not missing a beat, she replied, 'I need a TV so I can keep up with the news.'

"I told her, 'We have a big-screen TV in the living room. You can watch the news every single day.'

"Pat crossed her arms and said, 'Well, I can't come. I need my own TV.'

"I looked directly at her and said, 'If the lack of a TV in your room makes you refuse an address, a shower, and clean clothes, then your opening statement isn't true.'

"She scoffed, looking the other way.

"I then offered to keep the room open for twenty-four hours in case she changed her mind. Afterward, Pat left the meeting and never came to the mission."

"Wow, she has her needs and wants confused," Connie said. "Where did she go?"

"I have no idea, but she reminded me of Danny's mother. Both refused to listen or even attempt to be reasonable. They seemed to have some sort of mental barrier keeping them from making good choices. I feel sorry for them. Now they're chronically homeless."

"Do you think it's possible to help people who refuse to help themselves?"

"Well, we can't force them to stay in our shelter. Even if they come, we can't make them change. All we can do is create an environment showing God's love and offer resources that promote stability."

"What resources do you mean?"

I started to answer, but felt the need to get up. I walked across the room, recalling the conversation I had with the board three years earlier. I had suggested we give out material goods with caution, view them as a protective covering until the deeper wounds could be dealt with.

I turned and faced Connie.

"What resources do you think a person or family needs to obtain a house?"

Her brow flexed. "This might sound obvious, but it has to be some kind of money source. A job or savings account. Or property that can be sold. Maybe an investment or some kind of inheritance."

"Okay, let's call those things Material Resources. Anything a person owns or has access to, including money, would be a Material Resource."

I started pacing.

"Now, what resources would a person or family need to generate a home?"

"Well, that's altogether different," she said. "Since the people we work with have broken families, I suppose the greatest resource they could need is positive relationships."

"Yes. Like us, they need uplifting, encouraging people in their lives. Family and friends who will stick around in good times and bad."

Connie leaned back, rocking again. "They're a resource we didn't even know we had until today."

"That's true," I said. "We could call them Relational Resources."

"Sounds good to me. But do you think we're oversimplifying this? Why haven't others identified the lack of a home as the cause of homelessness?"

"Well, providing a home isn't that simple," I said. "You can't just hand Relational Resources to someone. Positive relationships take time and effort to develop."

"I guess that's true, especially for people who've never had them.

I paced the perimeter of the room, reflecting over Material and Relational Resources. I wondered if we were leaving anything out. Turning around, I faced Connie again.

"Can you think of any other resources we need to generate a home? Resources that help us become productive citizens?"

That instant, the back door opened and Rachel called out, "We're back."

"And we're hungry," Josh said, with Caleb and Sarah following him in. "Can we get a snack before youth group?"

Connie collected our empty glasses. "I can't believe our conversation with Clare led to all this. I hear noises upstairs, too. Jake and Ike must be awake."

I headed for the staircase. "I'll get the boys if you take care of the snacks."

"Fine with me."

On my way upstairs, I heard Connie chuckle and say to herself, "I guess it's time to take care of this home God blessed us with."

# TWENTY-FOUR

## Pyramid of Stability

That evening, after our children said their prayers and settled in for the night, Connie and I met in the living room once again. We looked forward to another opportunity for uninterrupted conversation, a rare treasure in our household of eight.

More important, we didn't want to lose the momentum of the day. Like a mosaic, thoughts and ideas we had formulated for years, were now fitting together for the first time. We could see a bigger picture forming.

"I've been thinking about your question," Connie said, noticing a fresh glass of iced tea by her chair. Her face brightened. "Thank you."

"Your smile is always worth it," I said in a melodramatic, yet sincere way.

She glanced at me, amused, and continued. "Earlier you asked if I could think of any other resources we need to generate a home. When you took the kids to youth group earlier tonight, I thought of one more."

"Great." I leaned back on the couch, ready to listen. Patch, our mostly black cat, emerged from underneath the opposite end of the couch and stretched. She ambled over to Connie, hoping to sit on her lap.

"I want to start out by saying I believe God is the greatest resource any of us could have. With Jesus, the written Word, and the Holy Spirit in our lives, we can have direct access to God and the wisdom he offers. That gives us the ability to make far better choices than we ever could on our own."

"You don't have to convince me of that."

She let Patch jump on her lap.

"So here's what I have," she said. "All of us have inner characteristics or traits making up who we are. We use them to interact with people and make decisions every day. When these traits are healthy and strong, they enable us to develop good relationships—allowing us to function well in life.

"I would call these traits Inner Resources, and they bring stability to our lives. They're the unique set of positive traits we carry inside of us that help us generate a home."

She picked up a piece of paper, referring to it.

"Things such as respect for authority, personal responsibility, a strong work ethic, moral values, intelligence, a sense of humor, resiliency, self-control, motivation, tenacity, reasoning abilities, common sense, a positive attitude, confidence, and of course, faith in God which brings love, joy, peace, wisdom, knowledge, insight, and so much more into our lives."

She patted the cat mindlessly.

"I wrote down more, but you get the idea. I put respect for authority and personal responsibility at the top since you always look for that in our residents."

"Yes, those two qualities show us who we can work with."

Connie handed me her list.

"I believe our Inner Resources determine how well we adapt in society and how productive we become as citizens."

She nudged Patch to the floor and picked up her tea.

"That's excellent," I said, getting on my feet. I strolled across the room, processing new thoughts.

"Inner Resources are God-given seeds of potential," I said, "and best developed in a loving environment by caring family members. Without positive people in our lives—Relational Resources—our seeds of potential can be damaged or ruined altogether. That's why growing up in a home is so important."

Connie, sipping her tea, watched me circle the room.

"A loving home encourages our uniqueness, and helps us understand our value and worth. Without a loving home, we go through life searching for meaning and purpose, unable to care about the people around us."

I made a leisurely lap around the room.

"Well, it's obvious," Connie said. "The people in our childhood have the greatest impact on our Inner Resources for good or bad. We see this with our own kids. They thrive on love and encouragement."

"They do, and the medical community validates this. I just read a medical study[1] the other day—I'll have to show it to you—that concluded love and bonding are the most important needs of babies and children. Loving parents have known this for centuries, and science is now confirming it through these studies.[2] That means Relational Resources are necessary for children to become emotionally healthy adults."

I strolled over by the couch, taking a drink of tea.

"Without caring people in their lives," I said, on the move again, "the kids grow up feeling unworthy and undeserving.[3] We see that at the mission. After years of being neglected, torn down, or violated in some way, these kids have no idea who they are. Their identity has been stolen.

"They have a hard time relating to anyone. They feel inadequate, and they know something is missing from their lives. They dream of a happy family, but like Clare, it scares them because they cannot trust anyone. 'Home' becomes an elusive dream."

Connie scowled. "The parents have no idea they're affecting their children that way. Or maybe they don't care."

"The vast majority are carrying their own pain and issues from the past. That's why negative behaviors get passed down to their children."

"Ugh. The cycle is frustrating and sad," she said.

I circled the room again.

I thought about the three types of resources we had identified: Relational Resources, Inner Resources, and Material Resources. An image came to mind.

I stood still.

"What?" Connie asked.

"It's a pyramid."

"What is?"

"The resources every person needs to become a productive citizen."

"And that means?"

"People cannot hold onto their *Material* Resources unless they have enough *Inner* Resources to make good decisions. And they cannot develop *Inner* Resources unless they've had enough *Relational* Resources to nurture and guide them along the way."

"Are you saying Relational Resources sit at the base of the pyramid?"

"Yes. Relational Resources would stretch across the base of the pyramid as the foundation since caring people are the most significant factor in our lives. Above that, would sit Inner Resources because they are nurtured and developed by Relational Resources. Then, at the top, we'd have Material Resources— which are the tip of the pyramid. The two resources underneath provide the stability needed to hold onto Material Resources."

"We had it backward for years," Connie said. "We tried to solve homelessness with Material Resources. We thought helping people find jobs, money, and housing was the key to stability. But it never lasted."

"That's because Material Resources aren't self-sustaining. We can see that now. They cannot stand alone. Without Relational and Inner Resources, they become fodder for foolishness."

Connie chuckled at my choice of words, but agreed. "Well, it doesn't take long for Material Resources to disappear in the hands of a homeless person. I suppose the solution for homelessness would be the reverse, right? Start at the bottom of the pyramid and work up?"

I felt a surge of energy. "Yes, we help people develop Relational Resources first, and then help them build Inner Resources. Once this happens, they can acquire and hang onto their Material Resources."

I began pacing again.

"I like the pyramid," Connie said. "It'll make an easy graphic when we explain this."

"I agree. I think we could call it the Pyramid of Stability."

"I like that name," she said. "Too bad we didn't understand all this sooner. How many people have we seen fall back into homelessness?"

A former resident came to mind. "Like Janetta?"

"She's the perfect example," Connie said. "I couldn't help but fall in love with her huge personality and smile. I think we all did. She never knew a stranger. I still can't believe what happened."

I returned to the couch, taking a drink of my tea.

"Money changed everything," I said. "After being clean for five months, Janetta received a disability check for $3,500 to cover her prior months of addiction. The government, without knowing it, funded her next colossal drug binge. That money lured her back on the streets."

Connie's eyes turned red. "I wonder if she's still alive. The last thing a drug addict needs is money or material goods that can be sold on the street. It's so frustrating."

"I agree, and as providers, we need to be careful how we help people in poverty and homelessness. Even with good motives we can cause harm. Showering them with Material Resources isn't the answer. Too often, the recipients use the resources to feed their addictions instead of their children. Then they have to come back for more. It's a perpetual cycle."

"The cycle isn't too surprising," Connie said. "Their relational wounds cause them to make the same poor decisions over and over. I feel bad for them."

"So do I, but the answer isn't more material goods. They need long term solutions."

"What about the people coming to us with physical needs? They still need basic necessities, don't you think?"

I had to get up for this. I crossed to the other side of the room.

"Any resources we provide, including shelter, must be used in a way that encourages the development of Relational and Inner Resources."

"You mean, motivate people in some way?"

"Why not? Many of the people we work with have very little reason to change. They've been hurt too many times. They've lost hope and don't want to try again. And why should they? Most of them receive enough Material Resources from agencies in town to survive without changing a thing."

I paced a wide circle.

"If we attach expectations to the Material Resources we provide, it could encourage them to develop Relational and Inner Resources."

"That's an idea," Connie said. "It might provide the incentive they need to climb out of their pain and addictions."

"I hope so. We need to pray about this more, but to answer your question, yes, we still need to provide basic necessities up front. Then, once their initial chaos is calmed, we can begin to lay out specific expectations for them to accomplish."

I felt my energy starting to wane.

"We have to make exceptions for the chronic homeless with mental limitations, but for everyone else, we can look at developing a set of expectations that promote Relational and Inner Resources."

"I'm glad you want to make exceptions for people with special needs," Connie said. "They may always need help."

"I agree, but even the limited folks have abilities that can be tapped into. Remember the Becker brothers? They had IQs in the seventies, but their parents lovingly pushed them to live above that. Today, they hold jobs and have their own families. They live productive lives."

Connie's brow creased.

"Not everyone can do that, Scott. We run into people who function at a much lower level, with mental issues that won't change outside of a miracle from God. If they had family taking care of them, it wouldn't be an issue, but the ones we see have dysfunctional or broken families. They hate the confines of a shelter and end up on the street. They're chronically homeless and a threat to their own health, and maybe to others."

"You're right, and those folks need long term help. They need a safe place to live that provides specialized treatment. Emergency shelters and streets aren't the answer."

With my energy gone, I went back to the couch.

"We aren't going to solve all the problems tonight," I said. "No matter what, we have to be more strategic if we want to help folks out of poverty and homelessness."

We relaxed for a moment, each in our own thoughts.

"I was wondering," Connie said, "wouldn't our mission be considered a resource itself, since we offer help to people in need?"

"Well, we're definitely an *outside* resource for people who hit rock bottom and cannot make it on their own. When they have to go outside of their circle of influence for housing or material goods, places like ours become an outside resource for them."

"Can we call ourselves Outside Resources then?" she asked.

"I don't see why not."

"That would include any agency, business, church, or non-profit helping strangers?"

"Yes, and individuals, too. Anyone helping another person in need—even dropping money in a panhandler's bucket—becomes an Outside Resource. Of course, panhandling can be a scam, but that's another conversation."

"It's too bad our country's benevolent system is so backward," Connie said.

"Yeah, people can't stabilize underneath their piles of Material Resources. Everyone, including the government, hands out money and material goods to people in need. The Pyramid of Stability has been turned upside down, and right now, it's acting like a top, balancing on its tip, spinning."

"You're so creative."

"What does a top need to keep spinning?" I asked.

"Energy?"

"And where do you think this top gets its energy?"

She looked puzzled.

"From Outside Resources," I answered. "All the churches, organizations, government agencies, and businesses who believe the same way we did when we first began in homeless ministry. Their vast supplies of Material Resources keep the energy flowing, the top spinning."

"Until their supply runs out," Connie said.

"That's when the top loses its energy and topples over, just like Elaine. When her Material Resources ran out, she spiraled downward. Everything looked great at first. Then it all fell apart. Money gave Elaine hope for the future, but it didn't last. She needed *more* money and *more* stuff to keep the spin going."

Sighing, I laid my head back.

"Success cannot be defined by keeping the homeless spinning year after year. We need to stop the spin and help people build a stable foundation. A home."

I closed my eyes, feeling drained. It had been a long day.

Connie noticed the clock. "Wow, it's midnight. The kids will be up in six hours. Maybe we should retire this discussion and go to bed."

"Nothing sounds better."

Forcing myself to stand, I offered my hand to Connie, pulling her up.

"We have a lot of work ahead of us," I told her. "I need to present this to the board in a couple of weeks. They've been waiting patiently on us for three years."

"At least you have something to present now."

Turning off the light, I had to agree.

*Thank you, Lord, for your revelation and clarity. Help us communicate the knowledge you've given. In Jesus' name.*

# TWENTY-FIVE

## Moving Forward

"After three years of praying and searching for answers, I believe we've found the root cause of homelessness."

The trustees held my gaze.

"I know this won't sound profound," I said, "but the missing factor in the lives of the homeless is a *home*."

Several smiled, yet waited for more.

"Every person we work with had housing at one time or another, but the vast majority never had a home with a caring family. For them, childhood was a stark, lonely existence filled with pain and rejection. Now, as adults, their memories haunt them, and they find it hard to relate to people and make good decisions. That's significant, because they cannot function in society long-term on their own."

For the next thirty minutes I talked about the contrast between a house and a home. Next, I described the types of homelessness found in our country: Traumatic, Self-induced, and Chronic.

Then I passed around diagrams of the Pyramid of Stability, showing the resources every person needs for lasting stability in society. I explained how Relational Resources are the foundation for Inner Resources, and how they both are needed to sustain Material Resources.

"I like the pyramid idea," the treasurer said. "The diagram makes it so much clearer."

"Me, too," another trustee said, "I can see how Relational Resources are the most important aspect of my life. When I was a boy, my family had few possessions, but we never felt poor. We loved and appreciated each other. I wouldn't be the person I am today without their love and encouragement."

Others agreed, sharing their own stories.

Afterward, Walter, our chairman, rested his hands on the table. "Sounds like you're on the right track, Scott. Now, what do you plan to do with this? What steps are you taking to make this information usable?"

He peered at me with unyielding, yet caring eyes.

"Well, I believe we need a team of people who can meet together weekly. If we work together, we can strategize and find ways to overcome homelessness. Then we can create a program that motivates people toward stability."

"How would you do that?" our oldest trustee, Roy, asked.

"Well, we would still provide basic needs when people come, and when their chaos calms, we would lay out specific expectations for them to fulfill. By that, I mean we would give them specific tasks and assignments that would help them develop Relational and Inner Resources."

I saw several nods.

"We want to link any resources we provide to their progress. By doing this, people will participate in their own recovery. We believe that will help motivate them toward stability."

Walter folded his hands. "That's the kind of answer I had hoped for."

Relieved, I felt three years of latent emotion wanting to surface. I tried pushing it back, but a deeper issue—one I didn't plan on bringing up yet—surfaced anyway.

I pulled out my handkerchief, wiping my eyes.

"We've had some bad news in our family," I said, trying to keep my voice steady. "Connie's mom has been diagnosed with stage four cancer. She's expected to live only a few months. Connie will need to spend time with her parents. She still wants to be involved at the mission, but I'm afraid she might have to cut back on her work for awhile."

Walter grimaced. "There's no 'might' about it. She needs to be with her mother. The way I read *my* Bible, caring for your parents is part of that *home* you're talking about."

I heard murmurs of agreement around the table.

"Several of us have been through that sort of thing," Walter added, "and it's never easy. Tell her we'll be praying for her."

My tears flowed now. I looked around the table, thanking God for these men and women who had become more than my bosses. They were part of my home.

*Thank you, Lord.*

Later that evening I shared the board's heartfelt concern with Connie, assuring her she could work behind the scenes at the mission while caring for her mother.

"Let them know how grateful I am," she said, wiping tears. "What about the team?"

"We have the board's support. They think it would be helpful having others come alongside."

She perked up. "You know, the first person we should ask is Elaine. Her passion and background would bring a great deal to the team."

"That's funny. She's the first person I thought of, too. She'll be lodge supervising in the morning. I'll ask her then.

The next day, I presented our proposal to Elaine. "The team will brainstorm in the beginning," I told her, "and after that, we'll begin the process of laying out strategies. If all goes well, we'll develop our program."

"Sounds awesome, Scott."

"Which brings me to a question. Would you like to be our first official member of the team?"

A huge smile spread across her face.

"Wow, I feel so honored. You know I'll do whatever I can to help people overcome homelessness." She leaped up, giving me a hug. "Thank you for asking me. Of course, I accept. I can't wait to start."

"You'll have to be patient. We can't begin until after the holidays. We're hosting a prayer conference at South Side in November. Which reminds me, can you help us? The mission is co-hosting this event with the church, and we could use your expertise with food."

"Prayer and food are my two favorite things," she said, "and not always in that order."

Her hoot echoed through the lodge.

"I'll be glad to help, Scott."

The next month we arrived at South Side on a Saturday morning in November to set up for the Prayer Conference. Other staff members from the mission had agreed to meet us in the parking lot. We all carried supplies in.

Clare greeted us at the front door, ushering us inside. She had recently accepted Jesus Christ as her savior and Lord, and was baptized at the church. Her excitement about life was evident— and she was thrilled to be helping with the prayer conference.

"How can I not help my two favorite organizations?" she said, with a husky laugh. She grabbed Connie's box, carrying it in for her.

We soon transformed the gymnasium into a coffee shop café. Under Connie's direction, we arranged the tables, putting on table cloths and centerpieces. After that, Elaine stepped and supervised the food and drink stations.

We soon finished and checked the room, making sure everything was in its place. With only a few minutes to spare, we split up and manned our posts. We spent the rest of the day serving food and refilling drinks for the attendees of the prayer conference.

During the conference, Elaine and Clare thanked me many times, saying how privileged they felt to be part of an event like this. I couldn't help but notice how happy they looked serving others.

*Thank you, Lord, for giving them a whole new outlook on life.*

The next morning on Sunday, we sat in the auditorium waiting for the worship service to start. We spotted Clare and Elaine sitting together near the front. Good friends now, they had much in common, sharing in each other's joys and sorrows.

The music began and both ladies jumped to their feet, ready to worship.

Connie and I watched as two ex-drug addicts danced to the wonders of a heavenly Father. The freedom they felt, arms raised toward heaven, was a sight rarely seen at South Side before their arrival.

I thought about the irony. Both of these ladies had scorned Christianity for years. Now they overflowed with God's amazing joy and peace. The perfect love of a heavenly Father had changed their lives forever.

Singing, I realized how much I had changed, too, and my eyes blurred with tears.

When Connie and I first began in homeless ministry, we had convinced ourselves it was a bridge to a larger, more significant ministry. Somewhere along the way, we discovered it wasn't a bridge at all, but a destination.

Only God, in his great wisdom, knew it would be a perfect fit.
*Thank you, Father.*

# TWENTY-SIX

## Homeward Bound

The following day, on Monday, I received a phone call at the mission. I picked up the receiver and heard someone sobbing. Trying to speak, the person only wept harder.

"Slow down," I said. "Take a breath. Who is this?"

I barely understood her next words.

"It's Carrie," she said, through muffled cries. "Mom's dead."

Elaine dead? That couldn't be right. My mind couldn't absorb it.

"What did you say?"

Carrie, heaving a breath, explained between sobs. "Kimi got back from basketball practice this afternoon…and found Mom dead in her bed. Maybe she was napping…I don't know…but she died in her sleep."

"Oh, no," was all I could muster. I didn't want to believe it.

I held the receiver, not speaking. Carrie wept in the background.

Minutes passed. Or seconds, I don't know. Time faded.

"Scott, are you still there? Can you come over to Mom's house? The coroner is on his way. I don't know what to do."

"I'll leave now."

"Please, hurry. I can't do this on my own. I need help."

I drove my car that afternoon, unaware of the route I chose or how long it took. All I could think about was Elaine at the prayer conference on Saturday. Enjoying every minute, she delighted in every aspect, especially the food. She loved cooking it, serving it, eating it, cleaning it up. Elaine turned our work into a party. She made people laugh, visiting, jesting with each person in line. Everyone felt welcome and wanted.

Never would I have guessed that weekend would be Elaine's final victory lap.

Driving to her house, I remembered a conversation we had two months earlier in the lodge office.

"I know my life will be cut short because of my drug use," she told me, "but I'm not worried about it. All I can do is live each day as if it's my last. I plan to enjoy my family and friends while I can and love them with all my heart. I talked to Sam about this, and he thinks I'm being morbid, but he promised to raise Kimi right if anything happens to me."

Elaine moved forward to the edge of the couch.

"I don't think I've said this to you before, but I want to thank you and Connie for caring about me. You guys never gave up on me, even when I let everybody down."

Her eyes filled with tears.

"You're welcome," I said, "but I don't want to think about your premature death. I know the doctor said your body is wearing out, but I'd like to think God has more plans for you here on earth."

Elaine smiled as tears trickled down. "It's amazing to think how different my life is now. I have so much more fun *sober* than I ever did when I partied."

She hooted in her usual, raucous manner. It's a laugh I will never forget.

In her short time with us, Elaine had influenced more people than most of us do in a lifetime. Her speaking venues had gotten larger and more frequent, and hordes of teens would crowd around her wanting more. Elaine's life and energy were contagious.

I thought she'd be with us longer.

I parked my car in front of Elaine's duplex, and Carrie met me at the front door.

"The ambulance arrived first," she said, sponging her face with a cloth. "The paramedic thought she died about four hours ago. The coroner just left. They've taken her, Scott. She's gone."

Carrie choked back a sob. "Mom looked so peaceful."

I gave her a hug and told her about the conversation I had with Elaine two months earlier, hoping it might bring comfort. She shed quiet tears, listening. Afterward, she hugged me.

"Mom knew her time was up."

We both nodded, trying to process our new reality.

Elaine couldn't be gone.

The coroner would later report she died of a grand mal seizure, the outcome of her many years of drug abuse. Elaine had been right. The drugs would demand their payment.

Driving home that evening, I thought about her transformation. Although her life here on earth had been cut short, her relationships were healed by the power of God's love. Now, her legacy would live on in the hearts of those she touched.

Instead of a funeral, we had a Celebration of Life service. Hundreds of people attended. The wealthy, the poor, the average, the broken, the comfortable, and the struggling. Elaine had bridged the gap of humanity with her life, and we all gathered to celebrate the precious gift we had received.

Standing by her grave, Connie and I said goodbye to a friend who had pushed us beyond ourselves. Elaine was the bridge we needed between her world and ours. Without even trying, she forced us to answer the deeper questions of life. Philosophical questions, that lay deep in our souls, only to surface when life summons.

How do we embrace a parallel world, sharing time and space, yet void of anything common or comfortable? Do we close our eyes and pull the cloak of familiarity over our heads? Or do we welcome this strange new world, allowing it to alter our emotional DNA? Do we risk opening ourselves up to astonishing growth, found just beyond our fear of the unknown? Or do we close ourselves off to protect the familiar and demand compliance to *our* view of the world?

As for Connie and me, we decided to risk our comfortable lives and take our children with us into the world of poverty and homelessness. Somehow, remarkably, along the way, God opened the door of understanding one lesson at a time, one person at a time.

Changing our lives.

That day, we walked toward our car after the graveside service, stepping carefully between headstones. Connie, carrying Isaac, held onto Jacob's hand. I held his other one. Together, we walked through the cemetery with our older children following.

At the car Connie lingered a moment, looking up at the sky. We all paused, noticing the brilliant hues above us.

Breaking the quiet hush of the burial ground, she asked, "Do you think Elaine is the only one dancing in heaven with Pink Panther slippers?"

We laughed, wiping our tears of joy and loss.

# EPILOGUE

In the world of poverty and homelessness, I found myself weeping at times. Not just for broken people, but for the countless blessings I had received in my life. I'd taken my world for granted.

The glaring contrast between a world full of heartache and darkness, against my world of love and laughter, was overwhelming and sobering. Even the simplest of childhood memories would bring tears to my eyes. Those memories, I realized, created the foundation of my life, the core of my being.

Yet it wasn't just the memories. It was the positive relationships I received as a child. Relationships I didn't have to work for, or give something up for, but were a gift. The idea that countless numbers of people never had these blessings was both revealing to me and humbling. I had to recognize, while being given so much, others received so little.

The world I grew up in seemed large and full of love. Now I could see how small and isolated it was next to the vast world of pain and brokenness. Stripped of my comfortable blinders, I had to face the harsh barrenness around me and recognize a truth: I carried within me a vast reserve of relational riches, the type of wealth a desolate people can only dream about.

So I had to ask myself, how can I possibly use my blessings to help others? How can I honor all those who had freely given to me?

That revelation wouldn't come easy.

Connie and I worked at the mission almost seven years before the significance of *home* took center-stage in our understanding of homelessness. Looking back now on those early years, it's interesting to see how long the process took, how many experiences we needed to change our thinking.

Our box of preconceived ideas—built with the sturdy walls of cultural influence—held up strong against the relentless reality we saw each day at the mission. Those walls didn't fall easily. They represented the "truth of the day." Everyone knows homelessness is about the lack of housing, jobs, and money, so why question it?

Yet, after hundreds of stories and thousands of hours working on the front lines of homelessness, we found a deeper truth.

The war on poverty in America has been won.

No longer do we have starving people who cannot get help. Our government, our churches, our local agencies, as well as our benevolent organizations, and caring individuals, have stepped in and filled this need.

Except the outcome isn't what we collectively hoped.

Instead of celebrating each other's accomplishments, both great *and* small, we've redefined poverty by raising the bar of "financial need" for every person. We've created an *illusion* of poverty. We ignore the fact that the poorest among us still rank alongside the wealthiest people in the world. Research tells us they're better off than nearly 70% of the people on our planet.[1]

Physical poverty isn't the real issue in America. Unlike famines and hardships found in third-world countries such as the Dominican Republic, our nation's poverty runs much deeper than anything material. It's a spiritual poverty, a *relational* poverty, reaching down into the soul, affecting every emotion, every decision, every connection in a person's life. No material bandage can heal the wounds of neglect, violence, and pain.

While people cry out for relationship—compassion, love, friendship—we're crushing them with a massive weight of Material Resources fueled by our "good intentions." Right now, goods and services pass through the hands of our poor at such a rate that obesity and entitlement flood our medical and social service communities.

The Pyramid of Stability has been flipped, and it's teetering dangerously. Our poor and homeless cannot hold onto their Material Resources because they lack strong Relational and Inner Resources. They're floundering in society without homes.

With this new focus, Connie and I set out to create a team of people who would meet together weekly for two years.[2] Because of her mother's illness and death, and then her father's, Connie couldn't meet with our team, but she stayed involved in the process.

Our team had two pivotal questions to answer. First, what do we initially see in the lives of people coming to our door for shelter? Second, what do we *want to see* in their lives before they leave? The answers would set our parameters.

Right away, our team identified the first answer. The vast majority of people seeking shelter come to us *shattered*. Every aspect of their lives is broken due to their lack of Relational Resources. Our hope is that, like Elaine, they recognize their condition and admit they need help.

Second, our team had to look at the endgame. What do these folks need to have when they leave? We unanimously agreed on *lasting joy and peace*, called *shalom* in Hebrew. We want everyone to find the long term stability that comes from having shalom in their lives, which comes through Jesus Christ.

So, with our parameters set, we began a course of action, developing strategies that could take a person from being shattered to finding shalom. This would become the basis for our program, *Stability for Life*.

Divided into three main phases, *Stability for Life* motivates people toward long term stability in society. On average, it takes a person up to two years to go through these progressive phases. We learned early on, life transformation isn't something we can rush.

The first phase, "Calming the Chaos," lasts up to six months. It begins the moment a person steps through our door seeking shelter. We found we cannot help people face the deeper issues of their lives unless they feel safe. Like Elaine, many are caught in a cyclone of chaos, which must be calmed first.

No one considers building a house in the midst of a hurricane, and this is the same idea. We cannot help people build a new life, a *home*, until they're willing to deal with their personal chaos.

The first thing we tell people moving in is, "Slow down, relax, and rest. Then sit back and watch our actions. Don't simply take us at our word."

In turn, we pay more attention to *their* actions than their words. Behavior tells us everything. We notice how they act and interact with others. Can they take direction? Are they willing to fulfill menial tasks and chores? Will they uphold our safe environment? Can they embrace a good attitude? Do they respect authority?

In this first phase, we begin to lay the foundation for Relational Resources. We introduce them to God, his Word, and the salvation he offers through Jesus Christ. We talk about God's love and forgiveness, how to receive it and extend it to others. We teach about good and bad relationships, helping our residents identify which ones to end and which ones to mend.

At the same time, we watch to see if they can take responsibility for their actions, and if they can show respect for others. If so, and they're willing to develop positive relationships, they can move forward to our second phase, "Promoting the Potential."

This phase, taking the longest, lasts up to a year. Here, we seek to develop and expand their Relational Resources while helping them cultivate strong Inner Resources. Individual mentoring, group classes, and self-studies are essential, allowing people to face their deepest issues while discovering who they are. Alongside this, we provide opportunities for personal growth.

Again, our highest goal is for people to find lasting joy and peace in—and with—God, themselves, and others.

In everything, we show the practical, relevant principles of God's love, while teaching his Word. We also show the benefits of prayer and why living an obedient, holy life through God's Spirit makes all the difference. Our hope is that hearts will continue to soften, and seeds will continue to grow as their knowledge of God increases.

Another area of priority in the second phase is *outlook*. How a person sees the world, what each person focuses on can either build up or tear down their ability to move forward. A good outlook sets the stage for a good outcome.

Once they complete phase two expectations and stabilize in the workforce a length of time, they graduate to our third phase, "Receiving the Reward." In this final phase lasting up to six months, we help them identify the potential snares of success while they continue paying off debt and saving money.

Their main goal now is to acquire stable housing in a safe neighborhood. With the finish line in sight, they now believe it's possible to reenter society as a productive citizen. During this time, we encourage them to find a good community that fulfills their spiritual and social needs. Community is key to their survival, so we encourage them to find positive places with strong relational ties that can last a lifetime.

We wish every person coming to our door would overcome homelessness, but that's not the case. Some aren't ready to change. And some never will. Others start the process, and then they decide to move out. They find it easier to live off the goodwill of others than to deal with their deeper issues and addictions. We don't consider them a failure. We know seeds are planted that can take root later.

We are still environmentalists.

The truth is, real recovery begins when dark meets light. An environment where God's practical, relevant love illuminates the starkest, darkest realities can change everything. In that atmosphere of love, we strive to give each person what he or she needs for lasting joy and peace.

Many of the people we work with, like Clare and Eddie Russell, have been ravaged by relatives or guardians who should have protected them. Their "caretakers" were so broken themselves, they could only plunder those around them.

Throughout the years, we watched Clare and Eddie's lives settle down and then get bumpy again. Their children carry many of their same issues. Although the Russells never went through a recovery process, they received much love and support from our local church and the mission. Amidst their many obstacles, Clare clings to her faith and the body of believers she considers *home.*

That, I believe, is our calling as the Body of Christ.[3] With Jesus Christ as our head, we are his followers working together as his "body" doing the same things he did. In this role, we come alongside "the least of these"[4] and show them what *home* looks like. We become their surrogate family, using Material Resources in a way that promotes Relational and Inner Resources.

In truth, it's not the government's job. They aren't equipped to handle the deeper relational issues of homelessness.

But the church is.

It's our birthright as the Body of Christ[5] to care for each other, to be relational. Yet we have somehow turned this over to the government. Now we must ask ourselves: Have we traded our God-given birthright for a shallower, easier version of the gospel?

One that brings instant gratification?

Are we handing out money, a cup of hot chocolate, a Christian tract—even a word about the good news of Jesus—yet failing to develop any kind of relationship that actually mentors, disciples, and compassionately delivers a person out of darkness?

That can get messy.

Yet that's what a loving Father in heaven asks us to do. He wants us to care for his flock, imitate the Son who stepped out of his perfect world to walk alongside our messy reality.

He wants us to long for a deeper understanding of the people brushing up against our world. He wants us to seek first his kingdom and his righteousness.[6]

And let him take care of the rest.

*Father, lead us into your kingdom of righteousness, joy and peace.*
*In Jesus' name.*
*Amen.*

# ABOUT THE AUTHOR

Scott and Connie Payne celebrate forty years of marriage and the raising of their six children, now grown, and serving the Lord. Their greatest achievement in life, they attest, is their family, which includes not only their children and spouses, but also their grandchildren, and their spiritual children.

*Unlocking a Broken World* is the Paynes' first book and testimony of how God's love invaded the lives of broken people. Prior to working with the homeless, Scott had spent six years working as the administrator of a Christian nursing home, and then four years as a full-time pastor. He is now in his twenty-ninth year at Inner City Mission.

Alongside his ministry positions, Scott served in his local church as an elder, and then as chairman of the elders. He also served on various non-profit boards as a trustee or chairman, and filled in as an interim minister and supply-preacher for area churches. He later became a consultant for new homeless shelters.

Connie, while raising their six children, worked part-time as the volunteer coordinator at the nursing home where Scott worked, and later as a pediatric dental assistant for four years. She then joined the staff at Inner City Mission in 1994. Her ministry roles at ICM have changed through the years. She began as a lodge supervisor, and then moved into case management. Later, she worked as the administrative assistant before becoming the director of operations for five years.

Connie is now the director of communications at ICM, writing and editing publications for Inner City Mission. Her interests include family, studying scripture, and creating art in its various forms. She enjoys reading, writing, journaling, painting, drawing, baking, sewing, health, fitness, worship, and prayer.

The Paynes are currently writing their program, *Stability for Life*, which they hope to publish and make available for others to use. They continue to enjoy their children and grandchildren, while still serving in the field of homeless ministry, and staying connected in the body of Christ.

# WHAT YOU CAN DO

1. Pray for broken people to find stability through:

   - relationship with God, Jesus, and his Holy Spirit.
   - positive relationships with others
   - the renewing of their minds through God's word
   - prayer and journaling
   - discipleship and training classes
   - deliverance from trauma, fears, addictions, bitterness, rebellion, shame, etc.
   - God's lasting joy and peace
   - emotional, spiritual, and physical healing

2. Pray for workers on the front lines of homelessness to:

   - show God's love, justice, mercy, and compassion in every situation
   - seek God's Spirit of wisdom and revelation daily
   - receive God-given strength, resiliency, and good health
   - retain soft, non-calloused hearts

3. Join us at www.innercitymission.net and find out more about:

   - helping the homeless find their way home
   - homelessness in general

- homeless ministry in Springfield, Illinois
- transformed lives

4. Invite others to read *Unlocking a Broken World*. Share this book with others so they can learn more about "helping the homeless find their way home."

5. Pray about getting involved in your local community and churches. Find out more about the greatest needs in your area, and how you can personally help.

6. Feel free to contact us at scott@innercitymission.net or connie@innercitymission.net. We will, to the best of our ability, answer any questions you might have about *Unlocking a Broken World* or homelessness in general.

# SOURCE NOTES

## CHAPTER 2

1. Quote about insanity: "Doing the same thing over and over, but expecting a different result." Commonly attributed to Albert Einstein.

## CHAPTER 3

1. Matthew 6:33 "But seek first his kingdom and his righteousness, and all these things will be given to you as well."

2. Romans 14:17 "For the kingdom of God is not a matter of eating and drinking, but of righteousness, peace and joy in the Holy Spirit."

## CHAPTER 4

1. Matthew 5:3 "Blessed are the poor in spirit, for theirs is the kingdom of heaven."

CHAPTER 7

1. Levitas, Michael, "Homeless in America," *New York Times*, June 10, 1990, http://www.nytimes. com/1990/06/10/magazine/homeless-in-america. html?pagewanted=all&mcubz=3

2. National Coalition for the Homeless Factsheet, "Who is Homeless?" National Coalition for the Homeless, 2201 P. St. NW, Washington, DC 20037; 202-462-4822, August 2007, http://www.nationalhomeless.org/factsheets/Whois.pdf

   National Coalition for the Homeless Factsheet, "Why are People Homeless?" National Coalition for the Homeless, 2201 P. St. NW, Washington, DC 20037; 202-462-4822, July 2009, http://nationalhomeless.org/wp-content/uploads/2014/06/Why-Fact-Sheet.pdf

3. Matthew 6:33 "But seek first His kingdom and His righteousness, and all these things will be given to you as well."

CHAPTER 8

1. Matthew 22:37–39 "Jesus replied: 'Love the Lord your God with all your heart and with all your soul and with all your mind.' This is the first and greatest commandment. And the second is like it: 'Love your neighbor as yourself.' All the Law and the Prophets hang on these two commandments."

2. 1 Corinthians 13:4–8a "Love is patient, love is kind. It does not envy, it does not boast, it is not proud. It is not

rude, it is not self-seeking, it is not easily angered, it keeps no record of wrongs. Love does not delight in evil, but rejoices with the truth. It always protects, always trusts, always hopes, always perseveres. Love never fails..."

## CHAPTER 9

1. "Lookin' for Love," original song by Wanda Mallette and Patti Ryan. Revised later with Bob Morrison. Recorded by American country music singer Johnny Lee in 1980.

2. John 3:16 "For God so loved the world that he gave his one and only Son, that whoever believes in him shall not perish but have eternal life."

3. Revelation 21:4 "He will wipe every tear from their eyes. There will be no more death or mourning or crying or pain, for the old order of things has passed away."

4. James 1:5 "If any of you lacks wisdom, you should ask God, who gives generously to all without finding fault, and it will be given to you."

5. Galations 5:16 "So I say, walk by the Spirit, and you will not gratify the desires of the sinful nature. 5:25 "Since we live by the Spirit, let us keep in step with the Spirit."

   I Corinthians 2:12-13 "We have not received the spirit of the world but the Spirit who is from God, that we may understand what God has freely given us. This is what we speak, not in words taught us by human wisdom but in words taught by the Spirit, expressing spiritual truths in spiritual words."

6. John 14:25-27 "All this I have spoken while still with you. But the counselor, the Holy Spirit, whom the Father will send in my name, will teach you all things and will remind you of everything I have said to you. Peace I leave with you; my peace I give."

   John 16:13-14 "But when he, the Spirit of truth, comes, he will guide you into all truth. He will not speak on his own; he will speak only what he hears, and he will tell you what is yet to come. He will bring glory to me by taking from what is mine and making it known to you."

7. Acts 2:17 [Joel 2:28] "In the last days, God says, I will pour out my Spirit on all people."

## CHAPTER 12

1. Acts 17:24-26 "The God who made the world and everything in it is the Lord of heaven and earth and does not live in temples built by hands. And he is not served by human hands as if he needed anything, because he himself gives all men life and breath and everything else. From one man he made every nation of men, that they should inhabit the whole earth; and he determined the times set for them and the exact places where they should live."

2. Acts 17:27-28 "God did this so that men would seek him and perhaps reach out for him and find him, though he is not far from each one of us. For in him we live and move and have our being. As some of your own poets have said, 'We are his offspring.'"

3. I John 4:7-12 "Dear friends, let us love one another, for love comes from God. Everyone who loves has been born of God and knows God. Whoever does not love does not know God, because God is love. This is how God showed his love among us: He sent his one and only Son into the world that we might live through him. This is love: not that we loved God, but that he loved us and sent his Son as an atoning sacrifice for our sins. Dear friends, since God so loved us, we also ought to love one another. No one has ever seen God; but if we love one another, God lives in us and his love is made complete in us."

4. I John 4:13-16 "And so we know and rely on the love God has for us. God is love. Whoever lives in love lives in God, and God in him."

## CHAPTER 14

1. "On the Road Again," original song written and recorded by Willie Nelson for the movie *Honeysuckle Rose*. It was later released as part of the album *Honeysuckle Rose* in 1980. Nelson received a Grammy Award for "On the Road Again" in the category of Best Country Song and was nominated for Best Original Song during the 53rd Academy Awards. The song was inducted into the Grammy Hall of Fame.

## CHAPTER 15

1. Luke 22:31–34 "'Simon, Simon, Satan has asked to sift you as wheat. But I have prayed for you, Simon, that your faith may not fail. And when you have turned back, strengthen your brothers.' But he replied, 'Lord,

I am ready to go with you to prison and to death.' Jesus answered, 'I tell you, Peter, before the rooster crows today, you will deny me three times that you know me.'"

2. Philippians 4:4 "Rejoice in the Lord always. I will say it again: Rejoice!" 4:7–9 "And the peace of God which transcends all understanding will guard your hearts and your minds in Christ Jesus. Finally, brothers, whatever is true, whatever is noble, whatever is right, whatever is pure, whatever is lovely, whatever is admirable—if anything is excellent or praiseworthy—think about such things… And the God of peace will be with you."

3. Romans 8:38 "For I am convinced that neither death nor life, neither angels nor demons, neither the present nor the future, nor any powers, neither height nor depth, not anything else in all creation, will be able to separate us from the love of God that is in Christ Jesus our Lord."

## CHAPTER 18

1. 1 Corinthians 3:5–7 "What after all is Apollos? And what is Paul? Only servants, through whom you came to believe—as the Lord has assigned to each his task. I planted the seed, Apollos watered it, but God made it grow. So, neither he who plants nor he who waters is anything, but only God, who makes things grow."

## CHAPTER 20

1. Matthew 5:11–12 "Blessed are you when people insult you, persecute you and falsely say all kinds of evil against you because of me. Rejoice and be glad, because great is your

reward in heaven, for in the same way they persecuted the prophets who were before you."

CHAPTER 24

1. Tomison, Adam, and Tucci, Joe, "Emotional Abuse: The Hidden Form of Maltreatment," Australian Institute of Family Studies, NCPC Issues No. 8, September 1997, https://aifs.gov.au/cfca/publications/emotional-abuse-hidden-form-maltreatment

2. Winston, Robert, and Chicot, Rebecca, "The Importance of Early Bonding on the Long Term Mental Health and Resilience of Children," *London Journal of Primary Care (Abingdon)*, vol 8(1) 12-14, February 24, 2016, https://www.tandfonline.com/doi/full/10.1080/17571472.2015.1133012 https://www.ncbi.nlm.nih.gov/pmc/articles/PMC5330336/

3. Children's Bureau Factsheet, "Longterm Consequences of Child Abuse and Neglect," Child Welfare Information Gateway, April 2019, https://www.childwelfare.gov/pubPDFs/long_term_consequences.pdf

EPILOGUE

1. Worstall, Tim, "Astonishing Numbers: America's Poor Still Live Better Than Most of the Rest of Humanity," *Forbes.com*, June 1, 2013, https://www.forbes.com/sites/timworstall/2013/06/01/astonishing-numbers-americas-poor-still-live-better-than-most-of-the-rest-of-humanity/#215ad15554ef

Kocchar, Rakesh, "How Americans Compare With the Middle Class," *Pew Research Center*, Fact Tank, July 9, 2015, http://www.pewresearch.org/fact-tank/2015/07/09/how-americans-compare-with-the-global-middle-class/

2.  Team members that met with Scott Payne to lay the initial foundation for *Stability for Life*: TyLinda Blackstock, Jeff Higginson, Rebecca Payne, and Dennis Petty.

3.  Ephesians 5:29–30 "After all, no one ever hated his own body, but he feeds and cares for it, just as Christ does the church—for we are members of his body.

4.  Matthew 25:40 "…I tell you the truth, whatever you did for one of the least of these brothers of mine, you did for me."

5.  1 Corinthians 12:12–14 "The body is a unit, though it is made up of many parts; and though all its parts are many, they form one body. So it is with Christ. For we were all baptized by one Spirit into one body—whether Jews or Greeks, slave or free—and we were all given one Spirit to drink. Now the body is not made up of one part but of many." 12:20 "As it is, there are many parts, but one body." 12:25-27 "…there should be no division in the body, but that its parts should have equal concern for each other. If one part suffers, every part suffers with it; if one part is honored, every part rejoices with it. Now you are the body of Christ, and each one of you is a part of it."

6.  Matthew 6:33 "But seek first his kingdom and his righteousness, and all these things will be given to you as well."

CPSIA information can be obtained
at www.ICGtesting.com
Printed in the USA
LVHW041440170921
698066LV00005B/11